WORLD OF
SCIENCE

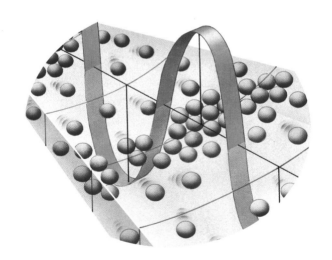

Acknowledgements

Model Photography
Mike Perry, David Lipson Photography Ltd

Models
Kate Birkett, Alison Cobb, Sam Connolly, Alexander Green, Jack, Robert and Sally Hutchinson, Karen Jolly,
Sian Liddell, April McGhee, Alice McGhee, Nicky Maynard, Ned Miles, Aaron Phipps, Joshua Phipps,
Katie Reeve, Nicholas Seels, Naomi Tayler, Chelsea Taylor.

Additional props
Vivienne Bolton and Peter Bull

Artists
Mike Atkinson, Julian Baker, Julie Banyard, Andy Beckett, Kuo Kang Chen, Contour Publishing, Ron Dixon,
Andrew Farmer, Mike Foster/Maltings Partnership, Jeremy Gower, Rob Jakeway, Roger Kent, Aziz Khan, Alan Male,
Janos Marffy, Gillian Platt, Terry Riley, Peter Sarson, Mike Saunders, Guy Smith, Roger Smith, Roger Stewart,
Techtype, Darrell Warner, Mike White, Alison Winfield

The publishers would like to thank the following sources for the photographs used in this book:
Page 6 (B/L) Mary Evans Picture Library; Page 15 (T/R) Dr Jeremy Burgess/Science Photo Library; Page 23 (T) The Stock
Market; Page 27 (B/L) The Stock Market; Page 31 (R) Dan McCoy/The Stock Market; Page 36 (B/R) The Stock Market;
Page 40 (T/R) The Stock Market; Page 45 (T/R) The Stock Market; Page 52 (T/C) courtesy BICC plc; (B/L) Science Photo
Library; Page 55 (B/R) Dept of Clinical Radiology, Salisbury District Hospital/Science Photo Library; Page 59 (B/L) Taheshi
Takahara/Science Photo Library; (B/R) The Stock Market; Page 68 (T/R) Leon Schadeberg/Rex Features; Page 69 (T/R) The
Stock Market; Page 71 (B/L) The Stock Market; Page 85 (B/R) courtesy Eurotunnel; Page 88 (B/L) NOAA/Science Photo
Library; Page 89 (C/R) Chris Bonnington Picture Library; Page 91 (B/R) SIPA/Rex Features; Page 92 The Stock Market;
Page 99 (T/L) Rex Features; Page 111 (T/L) Rex Features; (C) The Stock Market; Page 113 (T/C) Mary Evans Picture Library;
Page 116 (C) NASA/Rex Features; (B/L) Rex Features; Page 117 (T/R) SIPA/Rex Features; Page 120 (T/L) Claude Nuridsany
and Maria Perennou; Page 124 (B/C) Mike Vines/Photolink; Page 128 (B/R) B. Benjamin/The Stock Market.
All other photographs are from MKP Archives.

This is a Parragon book
This edition published in 2006

Parragon
Queen Street House
4 Queen Street
Bath BA1 1HE, UK

ISBN 1-40546-681-2
Printed in Indonesia

WORLD OF
SCIENCE

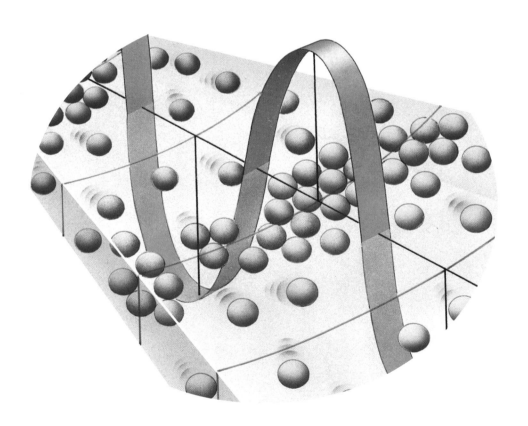

p

Contents

6 Introduction

**Section 1
Matter and Chemicals**

12 Atoms
14 Molecules
16 Solids, liquids and gases
18 Melting and boiling
20 Water
22 Dissolving
24 Chemical changes
26 Metals

**Section 2
Energy, Motion and Machines**

30 About energy
32 Converting energy
34 Forces and motion
36 Gravity
38 Heat and cold
40 Simple machines
42 Friction
44 Energy for the world

**Section 3
Electricity and Magnetism**

48 Electrical energy
50 Static electricity

52 Flowing electricity
54 Electricity from chemicals
56 Electrical circuits
58 Electricity makes magnetism
60 Mysterious magnetism
62 Communications

**Section 4
Sound and Light**

66 About waves
68 Sound waves
70 High and low sounds
72 Loud and soft sounds
74 Light
76 Reflected light
78 Refracted light
80 Using light

**Section 5
Earth and Life**

84 Inside the Earth
86 Volcanoes and earthquakes
88 Atmosphere
90 Weather and climate
92 Rivers and lakes
94 Life on Earth
96 Prehistoric life
98 Earth in trouble

Section 6
Space and Time

102 Earth in space
104 Exploring space
106 Earth's orbit
108 Inner planets
110 Solar wanderers
112 Outer planets
114 The Sun
116 About time

Science Projects

Matter and Chemicals

118–119 Mixing and diffusion
         Making solutions
         Growing crystals
120–121 Surface tension
         Capillary action
         Waterwheel

Energy, Motion and Machines

122–123 Hot-air balloon
         Aircraft wing
         Bernoulli's principle
124–125 Autogyro
         What a drag!
         Wind generator

Electricity and Magnetism

126–127 Conduct or insulate?
         Static electricity
         Making a battery
128–129 Magnetic fields
         Making magnetism
         A simple compass
         Radio waves

Sound and Light

130–131 Spreading vibrations
         Waves in a tray
         Two-ear hearing
132–133 How deep?
         Camera in a box
         Water-drop microscope

Earth and Life

134–135 Light for growth
         Phototropism
         Mould
136–137 What does fire do to air?
         The air and the weather

138 Glossary
140 Index

Introduction

WHEN DID SCIENCE BEGIN? Perhaps when early humans, more than a million years ago, picked up rocks and chipped them to form stone tools. Someone tried several different kinds of rocks. She or he noticed that a particular type of rock produced a cleaner, sharper edge than the other types. This was one of the first trial-and-error series of experiments. Gradually other kinds of rocks were tested and found to be even better. Materials scientists do the same today, formulating the latest metal alloys and tailor-made composites for special purposes.

Stone-age tools more than 10,000 years old show excellent crafting skills and an early knowledge of materials science.

Scientific method

Science is supposed to progress in a sensible, rational, step-by-step way known as the scientific method. We have an idea, a theory or an hypothesis. This must be in such a form that it makes predictions. We design experiments and tests to check the predictions. During the experiments we study, observe, measure and assess. We examine and analyse the results. If they fit the predictions, they support the original theory. After double- and triple-checking the experiments and results, we can move to the next stage.

A map showing the revolutionary ideas of Nicolaus Copernicus from the 1540s, that the Earth and other planets go around the Sun.

In this way we gradually build up a vast and interlinked body of knowledge and understanding, that stretches from the tiniest particles of matter, to the entire contents of the Universe.

Real science

The reality, however, is rather different. Science is not always logical and sensible, moving forwards in small, tried-and-tested stages. People have sudden insights and flashes of inspiration that can cause a scientific revolution. For example, Isaac Newton supposedly had his ideas about gravity when an apple fell nearby, perhaps even on his head. This simple event led to his theory of universal gravitation. It was so important that it formed a new foundation for the physical sciences for more than three and a half centuries. Then Albert Einstein brought yet another huge advance in the early 20th century, with his theory of special relativity, followed by his theory of general relativity.

The Great Pyramid of Giza in Ancient Egypt was built some 4,600 years ago, to an original accuracy of a few centimetres.

Fields of science

There are many branches or fields of science. In general, they fall into three broad groups. These are physical, chemical and biological.

The physical sciences deal with matter, energy, movement and the structure of the Universe. They are also concerned with machinery and technology.

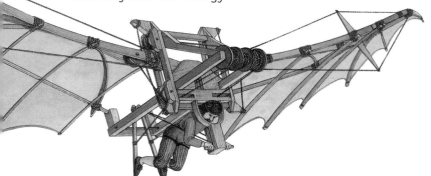

Leonardo da Vinci's idea for a flying machine (from about 1500) was never built and, in any case, it would have been far too heavy to fly. But it showed great scientific foresight and ambition.

The Industrial Revolution, which began in Britain in the mid-18th century, harnessed the power of machines for mining, processing, factory production and transport. Steam-powered railway locomotives began to puff across the countryside.

The brilliance of Albert Einstein (1879–1955) produced enormous changes in science. His ideas about gravity, time, space, particles and forces were fitted into the new framework of relativity theory.

Chemical sciences include the study of substances or chemicals (the chemical elements), what they are made of, and how they differ from each other in their many properties and features. Another very important area of chemistry is how substances or chemicals change when they combine or react together.

The biological sciences cover life and living things in all their forms, from microscopic germs to giant redwood trees and blue whales. They concern how they survive, move about, feed, breed and interact with their surroundings or environment.

Combined sciences

Traditionally, these three main branches of science were very separate. Today, they are usually found together. To make an artificial part or prosthesis for the body, such as a joint, requires all three branches to come together. The joint must withstand physical stresses and strains, chemical exposure to body salts and fluids, and biological contact with the body's microscopic cells. The sections in this book reflect the main branches of science, but also highlight the links and connections between them. The pages begin with the basic building-blocks of matter, atoms, and the forces that hold them together. They move to an ever-larger scale, ending with a look at the whole Universe and the nature of space and time.

Why do science?

Why is science carried out at all? To increase knowledge and understanding – although this

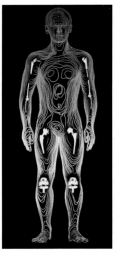

Biology, technology, materials science, engineering and design meet in the production of titanium-and-plastic body parts such as artificial joints.

The reusable space shuttles have launched hundreds of satellites and carried out thousands of experiments in the "zero gravity" of space.

The world shrinks daily as information transfer becomes faster and easier, using the science of telecommunications.

may not seem to be especially relevant to daily life. However, science has brought enormous changes to our modern world. We have hi-tech gadgets such as CD players, mobile phones, cars, planes, computers and the Internet. Most people live longer, more comfortable, healthier lives than ever before.

Yet our planet is at greater risk than ever before. Pollution darkens the skies and soaks into the soil and water. Our natural resources such as petroleum (crude oil) have almost been used up. Famine and disease are widespread in some regions. Playing with nature's genes could unleash a new breed of medicine-resistant super-bugs.

However, these are not the results of science itself, but of the way that science is used and applied.

In 1986 the nuclear reactor at Chernobyl, in the Ukraine, exploded and spread harmful radioactivity over millions of square kilometres.

Wealth and comfort in the industrialized world relies on land and resources which are often sited in less developed regions. Also the natural world suffers great damage.

Global warming, acid rain and ozone loss are just three of the major threats to our world environment.

1

Matter and Chemicals

All substances, matter and chemicals – from a pinhead to a star – are made of atoms. The atoms join or bond together to form molecules. Atoms and molecules can separate and then join together in new combinations. This is chemical change. Matter exists in three main states: solids, liquids and gases.

Atoms

BIG THINGS ARE MADE of smaller things. For example, a log cabin is made of dozens of logs. A log is made of millions of tiny fibres of wood. A fibre of wood is made of even tinier fibres of a substance called lignin. And lignin is made from groups of very tiny things indeed – atoms. Take apart any object, from a skyscraper to a pinhead, and you eventually find that it is made of these tiny particles, called atoms, which are far too small for us to see. All objects, items, materials, substances, chemicals and other forms of matter consist of atoms.

One kind
of atom

Another kind
of atom

Join or bond
between atoms

Different kinds of atoms

Atoms are not all the same. There are about 112 different kinds. These different kinds of atoms are known as the chemical elements. The names of some chemical elements are familiar, such as aluminium, iron and calcium. The names of other chemical elements are less well known, such as xenon, yttrium and zirconium. The atoms of the different chemical elements are all different from each other. So aluminium atoms are different from iron atoms, both kinds are different from calcium atoms, and so on. But all the atoms of one chemical element are exactly the same as each other. A lump of pure iron contains billions of iron atoms. Every one is identical to all the others. And they are all identical to every other iron atom, anywhere in the Universe.

Science discovery

Since ancient times, some scientific thinkers suspected that everything consisted of tiny particles. Democritus (about 470–400 BC) of Ancient Greece suggested the world and everything in it were made of particles, which were so small that they were invisible to our eyes. He believed that these particles were unimaginably hard, lasted for ever, and were always moving about. Parts of the modern theory of atoms are similar to the ideas of Democritus.

Atoms joined together

Sometimes atoms are on their own. At other times they join together with other atoms, to form groups of linked atoms called molecules. These are often shown as "ball-and-stick" diagrams or models.

Even elephants are atoms

Every piece and scrap of substance or matter is made of atoms. That includes the ground beneath your feet, trees, cars, houses, computers, compact discs, water and the invisible air all around us. All living things are atoms too, including birds, flowers, microscopic germs, huge trees, tigers, elephants – and your own body.

See also: Molecules page 14

Science discovery

John Dalton (1766–1844) was a science teacher who also kept detailed records of the weather. He suggested that every chemical element consisted of tiny particles, atoms, which were identical to each other but different from the atoms of other chemical elements. He also gave names and symbols to about 30 chemical elements. However, he thought that atoms were solid spheres, like metal balls, which could never be destroyed. Also, some substances which Dalton believed were elements are now known to be combinations of elements, or compounds.

Dalton's element symbols

- Hydrogen
- Azote
- Carbon
- Oxygen
- Phosphorus
- Sulphur
- Mangesia
- Lime
- Soda
- Potash
- Strontian
- Barytes
- Iron
- Zinc
- Copper
- Lead
- Silver
- Gold
- Platina
- Mercury

Atoms across the Universe

Everything in our world, including planet Earth itself, is made of atoms. And everything outside the world is made of atoms too. Space is not perfectly empty. It has bits and pieces of gases and dust floating about in it, and these are made of atoms. Objects in space, such as planets, stars and comets, are made of atoms. So are our own satellites, rockets and spacecraft. Most of the matter or substance in the Universe is inside stars, like our Sun. The main chemical element in stars is called hydrogen. So hydrogen is the commonest substance in the whole Universe. For every 100 atoms in the Universe, 93 are hydrogen atoms and only seven are of other elements.

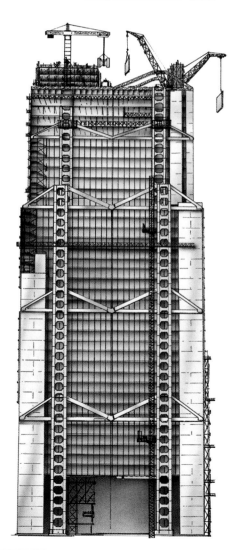

HOW BIG ARE ATOMS?

▶ Very, very small! An average atom is 0.000,000,001 metre (one millionth of 1 millimetre) across.

▶ Blow up a balloon. It seems to contain nothing and weigh almost nothing. But it contains about 100 billion billion (100,000,000,000,000,000,000) atoms of the gases which make up air.

▶ A tiny grain of sand contains so many atoms, that if each one were the size of a pinhead, the grain would be about 2 kilometres across.

Building blocks

A skyscraper is made of many smaller building units fixed together, such as steel girders, beams and panels. A house is made of smaller building units, such as bricks. Atoms are similar, but far smaller. They are "building blocks of matter".

Molecules

ATOMS ARE THE MAIN BUILDING BLOCKS of matter. But usually, they do not exist alone, each atom on its own. Atoms are generally joined to other atoms. When one atom joins with, or bonds to, one or more other atoms, the result is a molecule. Some molecules are made of atoms of the same element joined to each other. For example, the oxygen in the air around us is not in the form of oxygen atoms, each drifting about on its own. It is in the form of oxygen molecules.
Each oxygen molecule is two oxygen atoms joined together, written as O_2. Molecules made of the atoms of different elements joined together are known as compounds.

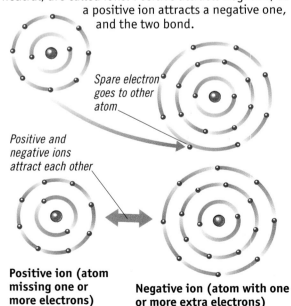

Nucleus of oxygen atom

Electron in inner shell

Shared electron swapping from one atom to another

Ozone

When three atoms of the element oxygen covalently bond to each other, the result is a tri-atomic molecule of oxygen, written as O_3. This is better known as ozone.

Electron in outer shell

Bonds between atoms

There are several ways that atoms can join together, or bond. One is the ionic bond, on the right. Another is the covalent bond, above, when atoms share one or more electrons. This happens because the various layers or shells of electrons in an atom can accommodate, or hold, up to a certain amount of electrons. The innermost shell holds up to two, and the next shell holds up to eight. If the outermost shell is not quite full of electrons, it can sometimes "borrow" an electron from another atom, and hold onto it part of the time. Likewise, if the outer shell of an atom has just one electron, it can donate this spare electron to another atom, but still hold onto it for part of the time. Two atoms which share one or more electrons like this have a covalent link or bond.

IONIC BONDS

Sometimes an atom can lose or gain an electron. This may happen when it dissolves in a liquid. If an atom loses an electron, which is negative, the whole atom becomes positive. Likewise, an atom that gains an extra negative electron itself becomes negative. Atoms which are positive or negative, rather than neutral, are called ions. Positive attracts negative, so a positive ion attracts a negative one, and the two bond.

Spare electron goes to other atom

Positive and negative ions attract each other

Positive ion (atom missing one or more electrons)

Negative ion (atom with one or more extra electrons)

See also: Dissolving page 22

Changing molecules

Burning is a chemical change. It happens when molecules break apart to release their atoms. Then the atoms join or bond together in new combinations. As a result, substances or chemicals alter into different substances or chemicals. When something burns, its molecules combine with molecules of oxygen, and give off light and heat.

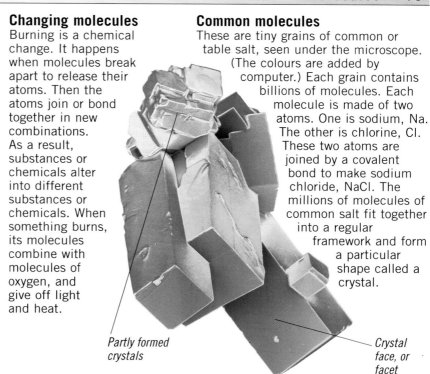

Partly formed crystals

Crystal face, or facet

Common molecules

These are tiny grains of common or table salt, seen under the microscope. (The colours are added by computer.) Each grain contains billions of molecules. Each molecule is made of two atoms. One is sodium, Na. The other is chlorine, Cl. These two atoms are joined by a covalent bond to make sodium chloride, NaCl. The millions of molecules of common salt fit together into a regular framework and form a particular shape called a crystal.

A supply of molecules

Molecules of oxygen and other gases float around in the air. They are so small, and so far apart, that we cannot see them. But we know they are there, because we breathe in air, to get oxygen into our bodies. Oxygen is a vital part of the chemical changes inside the body, which break down food to get the energy from it for the body's life processes. In water, we cannot breathe oxygen. So divers must take their own supply of oxygen, in tanks.

Changing places

At a huge event, people may wander about, to see who is there and what is happening. If they meet a group of people they like, they might sit together, stay a while and talk, then move on again. Likewise, atoms also move about. They link at certain times, by the process of chemical change, into molecules. Then they separate and continue their wanderings. Sooner or later, as a result of more chemical change, they join or bond with other atoms – and so on.

Solids, liquids and gases

MATTER IS ANY PHYSICAL SUBSTANCE OR OBJECT that exists in the three dimensions of space. It can be as huge as a planet or a star, or as small as one atom – or even as tiny as the sub-atomic particles inside an atom. Whatever its size, matter also exists in one of three main forms. These are solid, liquid and gas. They are called the three states of matter. A housebrick, lump of wood or sheet of steel are solid. The petrol for a car's engine or the oil for cooking food are liquid. A cylinder of oxygen in a hospital or an "empty" room contain gases. Each form of matter has its own features and properties. But the atoms and molecules in matter do not change for each different state. What changes is the way that the atoms or molecules can move about, or the way they are forced to stay still.

Changing states

The same matter or substance can change state, from solid to liquid, or from liquid to gas. These processes are called melting and boiling, and are shown on the next page. Another change of state happens when substances burn, or combust. In a vehicle engine, liquid petrol sprays into the cylinders inside the engine, along with air containing oxygen. The petrol catches fire and burns rapidly, combining with the oxygen in a mini-explosion. The result is not another liquid but a variety of gases. These leave the engine as exhaust fumes.

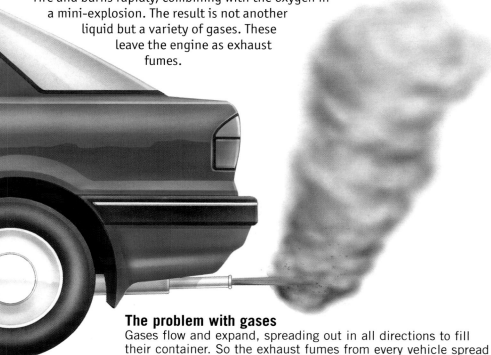

The problem with gases

Gases flow and expand, spreading out in all directions to fill their container. So the exhaust fumes from every vehicle spread out evenly through their container – the Earth's atmosphere. This is why pollution from vehicles is a worldwide problem.

See also: Atoms page 12, Melting and boiling page 18, Water page 20

Science discovery

Amedio Avogadro (1776–1856) worked as a lawyer before taking up science and becoming professor of physics. In about 1811, he imagined a row of the same-sized containers. Each held a different gas, but at the same temperature and pressure. Avogadro said that there would be exactly the same numbers of atoms or molecules in each container. This is now known as Avogadro's law – equal volumes of all gases, when at the same temperature and pressure, have the same numbers of atoms or molecules.

See-through solid

The glaze on a shiny vase is solid. Most solids are opaque. You cannot see through them. But clear glass, glazes and varnishes are see-through, or transparent. The glaze protects the beautiful colours and patterns of the paints beneath and allows them to show through.

THE FOURTH STATE

▸ The three main states of matter – solid, liquid and gas – have been known since ancient times.
▸ In the 1920s, a fourth state of matter was discovered. This is known as plasma.
▸ Plasma exists only at incredibly high temperatures, in nuclear power experiments, or inside stars.
▸ Small amounts of plasma also form in flashes of lightning.
▸ Plasma is like gas. But some atoms lose electrons and become positive, while the electrons move off freely.
▸ Charged particles such as these are called ions. So plasma is like a gas made of ions.

Swimming in the dry

Children enjoy messing about in a "ball pool". They can lie, roll, wade and swim. It's similar to splashing about in a real swimming pool of water, but without getting wet. The small, lightweight, hollow balls of the ball pool are like giant versions of the tiny atoms or molecules in a real liquid. They are free to move about. They flow when pushed around or poured out of a bucket. Also, like a real liquid, the balls cannot be forced nearer together or compressed.

Solid water

Solid water is called ice. In a solid, the molecules can move very little. They are held in a rigid framework or pattern by bonds between them. So a solid stays in the same shape, unless subject to powerful forces, such as twisting or crushing.

Liquid water

Liquid water is called – water! In a liquid, the molecules can move about fairly easily. This is why liquids flow and take up the shape of the container they are in. But the molecules in a liquid cannot be squashed nearer together or pulled farther apart, so liquids cannot be compressed or expanded by force.

Gaseous water

This is called water vapour. It floats in the air. In a gas, the molecules can move about very easily. This is why gases flow and take up the shape of the container they are in. But the molecules in a gas can also be squashed nearer together or moved farther apart. So a gas can be compressed into a smaller volume, or expand to fill its container.

Melting and boiling

MATTER CAN CHANGE IN STATE, from solid to liquid, or liquid to gas, or back again. This usually happens when heat energy is added to the matter. The heat gives extra energy to the atoms and molecules, which makes them move around more. When a solid is heated, eventually its atoms or molecules have enough energy to break free from their rigid framework. They begin to move around more freely, and the solid turns into a liquid. This is called melting. Each substance has its own particular temperature at which it melts. This is known as its melting point. Similarly, when a liquid is heated, at a certain temperature it becomes a gas. This temperature is called its boiling point. For pure water at normal temperature and pressure, the melting point is 0°C and the boiling point is 100°C.

Boiling hot
Each liquid has its own boiling point. Some cooking oils boil and begin to burn at more than 200°C, which is far hotter than boiling water at 100°C.

Under pressure
When a gas turns into a liquid, this is called condensation. This can be carried out by taking heat away from the gas, which is known as cooling. Or it can be carried out by compressing the gas – squeezing it to make it take up less space. The atoms and molecules of the gas squash closer together and change state into a liquid. They also receive heat so they become warmer. Huge ocean tankers carry natural gas compressed into liquid form, called LPG, liquid petroleum gas. This saves vast amounts of space.

Molten rock
"Solid as rock" is not always very solid. Even rocks melt if they become hot enough. Deep below the Earth's surface, the temperatures and pressures are so great that rocks are melted, or molten. They are known as magma. When they ooze or spurt out of a volcano, glowing and flowing, they are called lava.

Science discovery
Robert Boyle (1627–1691) was a chemist who did many practical experiments. He showed that for a gas which is kept at a constant temperature, then the pressure that the gas is under is proportional to its volume. So squash a gas into half its volume, and its pressure doubles. This is Boyle's law.

See also: Molecules page 14, Water page 20, Heat and cold page 38

Water-skating

Skating on ice is really skating on a very thin film of water. The blade of an ice skate has an upside-down U shape. Its two thin edges rest on the ice with great pressure. Increasing the pressure of a substance makes its temperature rise. So the ice melts into water for a split second as the skate goes over it. When the skate has passed, the ice then freezes again.

U-shaped hollow

Sharp edge of blade

Pressure melts ice to water

Only one edge of the blade touches the ice

Front view of ice skate blade

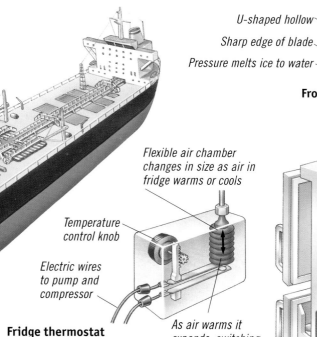

Flexible air chamber changes in size as air in fridge warms or cools

Temperature control knob

Electric wires to pump and compressor

Fridge thermostat (temperature control)

As air warms it expands, switching on cooling system

Keeping cool

A refrigerator uses the scientific principles of boiling and condensing under different pressures. A pump circulates a substance called a coolant in the pipes. The compressor outside the fridge compartment squashes the coolant. This makes it condense from a gas into a liquid, and also increase in temperature. Then some pressure is taken off the liquid as it flows through the evaporator pipes inside the fridge. The liquid boils, or changes into a gas, taking heat from the fridge's interior as it does so. This makes the interior cooler. The gas carries this heat out of the fridge and into the condenser pipes. It gives the heat to the surrounding air, becomes compressed into a liquid again, and so on.

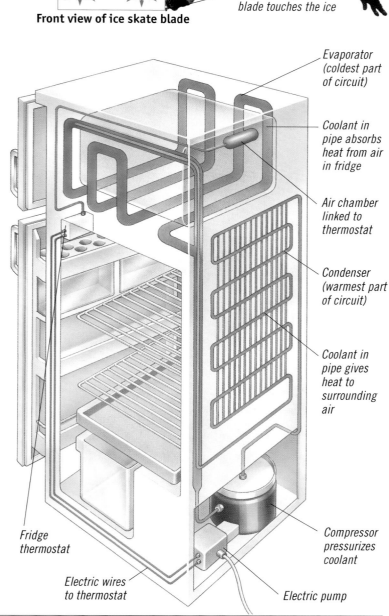

Evaporator (coldest part of circuit)

Coolant in pipe absorbs heat from air in fridge

Air chamber linked to thermostat

Condenser (warmest part of circuit)

Coolant in pipe gives heat to surrounding air

Fridge thermostat

Electric wires to thermostat

Compressor pressurizes coolant

Electric pump

Water

WATER IS VITAL for life on Earth. All animals and plants need water to survive. Those that live on "dry" land get their water from the soil or from streams, rivers, lakes, puddles, dew or raindrops. Water is also vital for our own lives. We collect and store water for drinking and washing, for our pets and farm animals, and for irrigating our crops. Each person needs to take in at least two litres of water daily, to stay alive and healthy. Like many other substances, water can exist in three different states. Water is the liquid form. Ice is the solid form. Water vapour is the gaseous form. All of these states occur naturally, with ice in cold places and invisible water vapour in the air around us. The natural steam belching from hot springs or geysers is water vapour mixed with tiny floating droplets of hot water.

Floating ice
Most substances enlarge or expand as they heat up, and become smaller or contract as they get colder. But water is unusual. It contracts as it cools down to 4°C. Then, as it gets even colder and freezes into ice, it expands again. This means a lump of ice at 0°C weighs less than the same-sized lump of water at, say, 10°C. So ice – from an ice cube in a drink to a giant iceberg in the ocean – floats on water.

Flowing along a pipe
Liquids such as water flow along channels and through tubes and pipes. But the flow is not smooth and even. The regions of water next to the channel's or pipe's inner surface move more slowly, because they rub against the surface. The region of water in the centre of the channel or pipe flows faster. This variation in speed of movement is called laminar flow. The same happens in a river. Water near the bank flows more slowly than water in the middle. The study of flowing liquids is important in the branch of science and engineering called hydraulics. This deals with how fluids flow and transmit pressures along pipes.

Science discovery
Daniel Bernoulli (1700–1782) was an expert in medicine, animals, plants, physics and mathematics. He showed that as water or another liquid flows from a wide pipe into a narrower one, the speed of flow becomes faster – and the liquid also has less pressure. This applies to flowing gases like air, too. This effect is known as Bernoulli's principle. It is used in many kinds of engineering and technology, such as the design of aircraft wings, so they provide a lifting force as they move through the air.

Flow disturbed by bend in pipe

Eddies (whirlpools) at corner

Fast flow in centre

Slow flow near edge

Bend in pipe makes water change direction

Laminar flow restored

See also: Solids, liquids and gases page 16, Melting and boiling page 18

Water for life

An oasis is a small area of water in an otherwise dry place, a desert. The water may be on the surface, as a pool or lake, or underground and reached by plants' roots or our wells. Life can exist in and near the oasis, but not in the desert beyond.

Cirrus clouds (ice crystals)

Cumulonimbus cloud (thunderstorm)

Water molecules

The smallest particle or molecule of water is made of two atoms of hydrogen (H) and one atom of oxygen (O), combined to form H_2O. The molecule has a particular shape, called a dipole. The two links or bonds between the atoms are at an angle of 105° to each other.

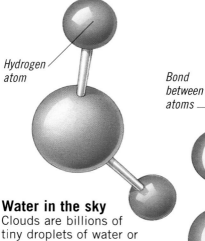

Hydrogen atom

Bond between atoms

Oxygen atom

Water in the sky

Clouds are billions of tiny droplets of water or crystals of ice. These are so light that they float.

FLOATING AND SINKING

An object floats because it weighs less than the water it pushes aside, or displaces. A huge ship may be made of heavy metal, but it also contains lots of air. So overall, it is lighter than a lump of water of the same volume. So it floats. A submarine can alter its weight by taking in water to make itself heavier, and dive. To rise again it blows the water out with air from compressed air tanks. This makes it lighter and it floats.

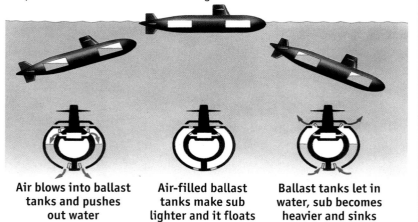

Air blows into ballast tanks and pushes out water

Air-filled ballast tanks make sub lighter and it floats

Ballast tanks let in water, sub becomes heavier and sinks

Water energy

Moving objects and substances have the energy of motion, kinetic energy. So water flowing downhill, pulled by gravity, has kinetic energy. This can be harnessed and turned into electricity in a hydro-electric power station. The energy of a very steep flow of water, the waterfall, wears away the solid rock below.

Dissolving

STIR SUGAR GRAINS into a glass of clear, clean water. They swirl around for a while, then they seem to fade away. Finally they disappear. But if you sip the water, you can still taste the sugar. It has not disappeared – it has dissolved. Its crystals have become smaller, gradually breaking up into their individual molecules or atoms. These are too small to see, but they are present, floating about among the molecules of water. The substance that dissolves – in this case, sugar – is called the solute. The substance it dissolves in – again, in this case, water – is known as the solvent. The two together, the solute in the solvent, make up a solution. In daily life, water is the most common solvent.

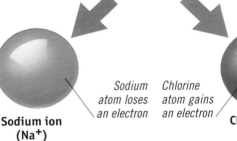

Molecule of two atoms joined together, such as common salt molecule, sodium chloride (NaCl)

Dissolve molecule in water and it splits into separate particles

Sodium atom loses an electron

Chlorine atom gains an electron

Sodium ion (Na$^+$)

Chlorine ion (Cl$^-$)

Hotter means more

The warmer a liquid, the more solute can dissolve in it. So you can dissolve more spoonfuls of sugar in a hot drink than in a cold drink. In the cold drink, undissolved sugar settles on the bottom.

Atoms to ions

When some substances dissolve, they change slightly. Their atoms are no longer neutral, that is, neither positive nor negative. One group of atoms loses their electrons, which are negative, so the atoms become positive. Another group of atoms gains the extra electrons, so they become negative. These particles are no longer known as atoms, but as ions. The positive ions are called cations. The negative ones are termed anions. The formation of ions is very important for all kinds of chemical changes and reactions, and also for producing or using electricity, as shown later in the book.

Dangerous dissolving

There are hundreds of kinds of solvents. Some, like water, are fairly harmless. But the powerful chemical solvents used in industry are not. They dissolve many substances, including our skin and flesh!

Dissolved in the sea

The clean, fresh water from our taps contains very little dissolved substances, apart from those added to kill germs and make it safe. But one sip of sea water shows that it contains dissolved salt. This is the same type of salt as common or table salt, sodium chloride. Sea water also contains many other dissolved substances, including calcium, sulphate and carbonate.

See also: Molecules page 14, Water page 20, Electricity from chemicals page 54

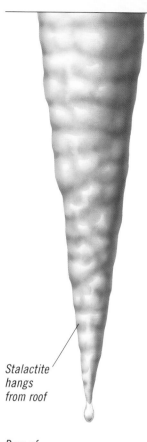

Stalactite hangs from roof

Drop of water full of dissolved minerals

Stalagmite sticks up from floor

Oil molecules gathered in clumps

Oil molecule

Detergent makes clumps smaller

Dissolving oil
Usually oil does not dissolve in or mix with water. The molecules of oil clump together into drops and float about on the water. But a detergent alters the features of water and makes it a more powerful solvent. It makes the oil drops break up into smaller and smaller clumps, which is called dispersing the oil. We use different types of detergents to wash our clothes, our cooking pots and pans, our eating crockery and cutlery, and also (in the form of soaps, foams and gels) our own bodies. Strong detergents disperse polluting oil slicks.

No more dissolving
Only a certain amount of solute can dissolve in a solvent. A solution which is full of solute is called a saturated solution. Saturation varies with temperature. A hot liquid can hold more dissolved solute than a cold liquid. As a warm saturated solution cools, some of the solute comes out of solution, and reappears as a solid again.

Out of solution
As rain water soaks into the soil and trickles down through tiny cracks in the rocks, it dissolves some of the natural minerals in the soil and rocks. It becomes a mineral solution. Sometimes this solution drips slowly from a cave roof onto the cave floor. As each drip of water falls, it leaves behind its minerals. Over thousands of years the minerals build up into sharp icicle-like shapes of rock – stalactites and stalagmites.

Coloured solute
Some paints are solutions. The solute is the coloured substance, pigment. As the paint dries, the solvent turns into a gas or vapour and floats away. The pigment particles remain as a coloured layer of paint.

Chemical changes

ATOMS ARE NOT FIXED into their molecules for ever. Molecules can come apart, and their atoms then join together again in new, different combinations. This is called chemical change. The atoms in molecules of one or more substances break their links or bonds with each other. They "shuffle their partners" and form links or bonds with other, different atoms. The result is one or more new substances, with different chemical features and properties compared to the original substances. Chemical changes need energy, such as heat, light or electricity, to happen.

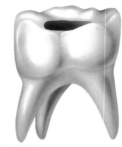

Tooth filling
The silver metal mercury is normally a liquid. But mercury combined with other metals forms an amalgam that sets very hard, for use in dental fillings.

Colour change

In chemistry, an indicator is a substance that changes colour according to the chemical conditions. A common example is litmus, used to find out if a substance is acidic or alkaline. The molecules of litmus undergo chemical change when exposed to an acid or alkali. The new molecules have a different colour, so the change is easily visible.

Paper strip containing litmus dye

Neutral (neither acidic nor alkaline) – litmus is unaffected

Acid turns strip red

Acidic – litmus turns red colour

Strip becomes blue

Alkaline – litmus turns blue colour

Fiery change

A familiar chemical change is combustion, or burning. When a substance catches fire, atoms in its molecules break apart from one another. Some link or bond with oxygen in the air. For instance, when wood or coal burn, the carbon atoms in the wood or coal break apart from their molecules and join with oxygen. They form a new substance, carbon dioxide, CO_2. One way of stopping combustion is to prevent oxygen – usually, from air – reaching the fire. A fire blanket or smothering foam does this. The chemical change of joining with oxygen stops, and the fire goes out.

See also: Molecules page 14, Light page 74

CHEMICAL BUILDING BRICKS
In a toy building kit, each brick or other shape is a single unit. Likewise, atoms are single units. Bricks fit together or join to each other. In the same way, atoms link or bond to each other. Lots of different bricks fit together to make a certain object, like an aeroplane. Similarly, different atoms fit together too, to form molecules of a certain substance. The bricks can be taken apart and then put together in a different combination or pattern, to make another object, like a house. Atoms in the molecules of one substance can be taken apart from each other, then reassembled to form molecules of a new, different substance, with different chemical features and properties. This is chemical change.

Bricks make up an aeroplane

Same bricks build a house

Science discovery

Henry Cavendish (1731–1810) was exceptionally shy, worked alone, had great wealth, yet rarely spent it. But he made important scientific discoveries. He produced water by exploding oxygen and hydrogen gases together. This caused a chemical change, joining one oxygen atom to two hydrogen atoms. He showed water was a chemical compound, H_2O, not an element as others believed.

Sticky change
An adhesive or glue is used for sticking things together. When it comes out of the tube, it is usually in liquid form. In one type of adhesive, as the liquid "dries", it does not simply turn from liquid to solid. Its molecules undergo chemical change. Their atoms separate from each other, lock into the atoms and molecules of the item being glued, then turn into a solid. In another type of adhesive, resin from one tube is mixed with hardener from another tube. The two seep into the surfaces being joined, and chemically combine or react with each other to bond the surfaces together.

Liquid adhesive turns solid

All change
A high tech object, such as a Grand Prix racing car, is the result of thousands of chemical changes. The metals in the engine parts were once combined with other minerals, in rocks. They have been extracted and purified, and combined with other metals to form alloys with special properties, such as light weight and great strength. The rubber in the tyres was extracted from rubber trees, then heated and chemically combined with other substances, in the process called vulcanizing. This makes it tougher, more elastic and hard-wearing. The plastic parts were made by chemically changing the raw ingredients in natural petroleum, or crude oil.

Metals

THERE ARE about 112 known chemical elements. More than three-quarters are metals. A typical metal is hard and shiny, tough and strong, and it conducts or carries electricity and heat well. Metals have thousands of uses in daily life. Often they are mixed or combined with other metals or substances, to form alloys. Almost any machine or device has at least one metal in it. The most widely used metal is iron, but not in its pure form. It is combined with small amounts of the non-metal carbon, to form the group of alloys known as steels. Making alloys is extremely important in industry. Often, alloys of a metal are harder and stronger than the pure metal itself. The science of metals is called metallurgy.

Strong as steel

The world's industries use millions of tonnes of steels each year. Steel plate forms the large panels in washing machines, cars, trains and ships. The stainless steel used for making cutlery and cooking utensils is an alloy with at least one-tenth of the extremely hard, shiny metal known as chromium. Steels with titanium in them form the light but stiff structural sheets in high-speed aircraft. Steel girders make the strong frameworks of skyscrapers, bridges and similar big structures. Other elements mixed with iron to form steels include manganese, phosphorus, silicon and sulphur.

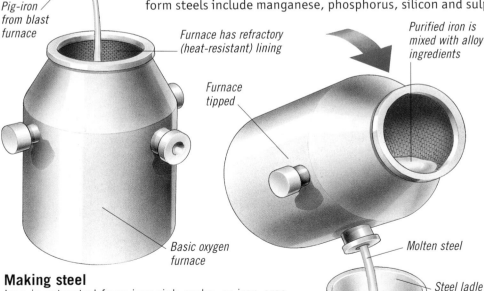

Pig-iron from blast furnace

Furnace has refractory (heat-resistant) lining

Furnace tipped

Purified iron is mixed with alloy ingredients

Basic oxygen furnace

Molten steel

Steel ladle

Molten steel is poured out as brick-shaped ingots to cool

Most valuable metal?
Gold is a famous symbol of wealth. But rarer metals such as platinum and palladium command higher prices for specialized engineering and electronic uses.

Making steel

Iron is extracted from iron-rich rocks, or iron ores, in a blast furnace. The result is pig-iron, which contains various impurities. These are removed by blowing oxygen through the pig-iron, a method known as the basic oxygen process. The steel is so hot that it is in melted or molten form, as a liquid.

See also: Solids, liquids and gases page 16

Aluminium

Also called aluminum, this is the most abundant metal on planet Earth (and the third most abundant of all chemical elements). It forms about one-twelfth by weight of the Earth's outer layer, the crust. Pure aluminium is very light but not especially strong. However, combined with other elements, such as copper, magnesium or silicon, it forms extremely strong alloys. Also it does not rust, unlike steel. Aluminium is used for making aircraft, ships, cooking utensils such as saucepans, drinks cans, cooking foil and take-away food cartons.

Silvery-white aluminium does not rust

Cans decorated and filled

Cans punched from thin sheet

Cans used, but not thrown away

Cans collected and partly crushed to save space

Recycling metals

Most metals occur combined with minerals and other substances, spread through rocks known as ores. It takes huge amounts of time and energy to dig or mine the ores, and then extract and purify the metals from them. Recycling helps to reduce these problems. For example, recycled aluminium uses only one-twentieth of the energy which is needed to produce aluminium from its ore. Many other metals can also be recycled, including irons and steel, and even the silver and gold used in electrical circuits – and false teeth!

Can to can

The entire journey around the aluminium recycling circuit, from being a drinks can to another drinks can, may be as short as one month.

Molten aluminium cooled and pressed into thin sheet

Thousands of cans compressed into large bale

Bales melted to produce molten aluminium

Unsightly mines

Mining metals from surface rocks, known as open-cast mining, can be very unsightly and scar the landscape for hundreds of years.

METALS THROUGH HISTORY

- One of the earliest alloys was bronze, a mix of copper and tin. It has been known for thousands of years and was the first widely used substance for tools, after rocks and stones.
- Brass is another common alloy, of copper and zinc.
- Perhaps the most famous metal is gold. It has been valued and cherished since ancient times because it stays bright and shiny, yet is also easy to work with.
- Silver is another long-valued metal. It is the best conductor of electricity of any metal. Silver is also used in jewellery, photographic film and for coins.

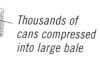

2

Energy, Motion and Machines

Energy is the ability to make things happen and cause changes. It exists in many forms, such as sound, light, electricity and chemicals. Moving objects also possess a type of energy, kinetic energy. Using energy and principles of mechanics and movement, we combine simple machines, such as levers and wheels, into enormously complex ones.

About energy

YOU CAN'T SEE ENERGY. You can't touch it or hold it in your hand. But energy is everywhere. Energy is the ability to do work, to make things happen and to cause changes. There are many different types, or forms, of energy. A hot drink has heat energy. A flash of lightning during a thunderstorm has both electrical and light energy. A lion's roar is sound energy. A racing car speeding around the track has movement energy, which is also called kinetic energy. Even a book lying on a shelf has energy. Because of its position and the pull of gravity, it presses down on the shelf. This type of energy is called potential energy.

Pictures from energy

Machines called scanners make pictures of the insides of the body. They send invisible waves of energy into the body and measure how these waves change as they pass through, or bounce off, the different body parts. A computer then analyses the strengths and directions of the changed waves, and builds up a picture or image. The image on the right of the brain and head was made using the type of scanner called a Magnetic Resonance Imaging, or MRI, scanner.

Radio energy

Radio and television programmes are received by aerials, which pick up invisible waves of energy sent out by transmitters. The waves consist of electrical and magnetic energy, so they are called electromagnetic waves. Some transmitters are fixed to the tops of tall towers, so that the radio waves of energy they send out can travel very long distances.

FORMS OF ENERGY

- Chemical energy, contained in atoms and molecules.
- Kinetic energy, in moving objects.
- Potential energy, from an object's position.
- Sound energy, when atoms or objects vibrate.
- Nuclear energy, when atoms join or split apart.
- Electrical energy, from moving electrons.
- Magnetic energy, due to magnetic attraction.
- Electromagnetic energy, in the form of various kinds of rays or waves. These include radio waves, microwaves, heat, light, X-rays and gamma rays.

See also: Mysterious magnetism page 60, The Sun page 114

Energy from the Sun

The energy we receive from the Sun is called solar energy. It consists mainly of light and heat that travel through space. These forms of energy come from atoms smashing into each other in the centre of the Sun and joining together, or fusing. This process is called nuclear fusion. Energy that comes from the centres or nuclei of atoms is called nuclear energy. The form of nuclear energy in nuclear power stations here on Earth comes from nuclear fission, when atoms split apart.

Soaraway energy

A ski jumper soars into the sky, leaning forwards to cut through the air and fly as far as possible. The jumper gets the energy needed for such a huge leap by sliding down a tall hill faster and faster, changing potential energy into kinetic energy, then leaping from the upturned take-off ramp.

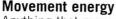

Energy for robots

Vehicle-building robots need energy to move their mechanical arms. This is usually supplied by electricity, which drives electric motors, which tilt and swivel the arms. The movements are controlled with great precision by computer.

Movement energy

Anything that moves has kinetic energy. The faster it moves and the more substance or matter (mass) it contains, the more kinetic energy it has. A fast train speeding across the countryside has an enormous amount of kinetic energy.

Science discovery

Hermann Helmholtz (1821–1894) developed the law of conservation of energy. It says that energy is never created or destroyed. It is simply changed from one form to another. Helmholtz studied various forms of energy, including the newly discovered radio waves. He was also a mathematician and medical researcher.

Converting energy

ENERGY CANNOT BE MADE or destroyed. It can only be converted. When anything moves or alters in any way, energy changes its form. A ball at the top of a hill has potential energy because of its position. As it rolls down the hill, some of its potential energy is converted into kinetic or movement energy. When a piece of wood burns, chemical energy stored inside its molecules changes into heat and light energy, and even some sound energy too, as the fire crackles. So energy is constantly changing forms, all around us. One simple event may involve a whole chain of energy conversions.

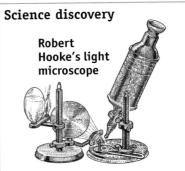

Science discovery

Robert Hooke's light microscope

Robert Hooke (1635–1703) suggested that light might be made of waves of energy. More than two hundred years later, this idea came to be accepted. He also studied how a coiled spring stores a form of energy, called potential energy, as it is stretched. Hooke was a skilled technician and microscopist. He invented and designed many instruments and devices, including his own microscopes and the universal joint now used in cars and other vehicles.

Steam power

A steam train is really solar-powered. Millions of years ago, plants trapped the Sun's light energy, converted it into chemical energy, then died and changed into coal. Burning coal converts this chemical energy into heat, which boils water to make high-pressure steam, which turns the train's wheels.

Generating electricity

A power station produces electricity by changing the energy in its fuel into electrical energy. A gas-fired power station burns gas, converting its chemical energy into heat. The burning gas expands and tries to rush out in all directions – it has kinetic energy. It turns the blades of a turbine, which drives a generator to make electricity. The hot gas also turns water into steam, which drives another turbine and generator. Condensers change the steam back into water so that it can be used again.

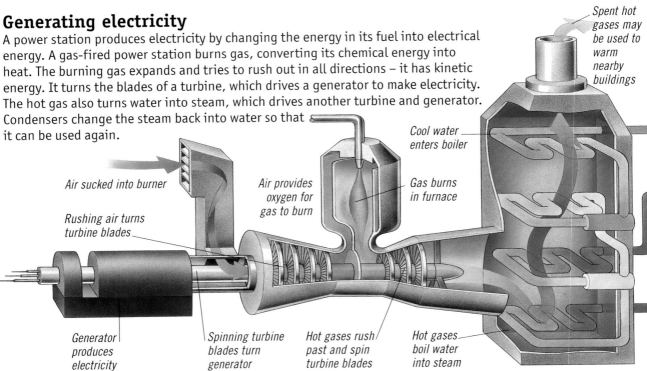

Spent hot gases may be used to warm nearby buildings

Cool water enters boiler

Gas burns in furnace

Air sucked into burner

Air provides oxygen for gas to burn

Rushing air turns turbine blades

Generator produces electricity

Spinning turbine blades turn generator

Hot gases rush past and spin turbine blades

Hot gases boil water into steam

See also: Molecules page 14, Light page 74

Solar panels

A satellite needs electricity to power its instruments, cameras and radio equipment. Most satellites get electricity from their solar panels. Each panel is covered by thousands of solar cells, which change sunlight directly into electricity. Some of the electrical energy is stored in chemical form, in rechargeable batteries.

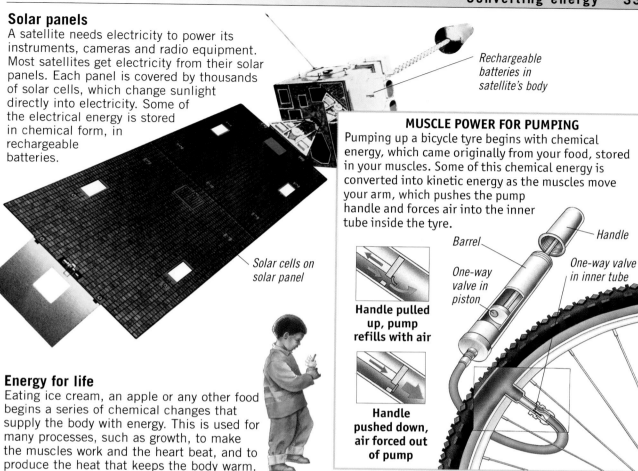

Rechargeable batteries in satellite's body

Solar cells on solar panel

MUSCLE POWER FOR PUMPING

Pumping up a bicycle tyre begins with chemical energy, which came originally from your food, stored in your muscles. Some of this chemical energy is converted into kinetic energy as the muscles move your arm, which pushes the pump handle and forces air into the inner tube inside the tyre.

Barrel

Handle

One-way valve in piston

One-way valve in inner tube

Handle pulled up, pump refills with air

Handle pushed down, air forced out of pump

Energy for life

Eating ice cream, an apple or any other food begins a series of chemical changes that supply the body with energy. This is used for many processes, such as growth, to make the muscles work and the heart beat, and to produce the heat that keeps the body warm.

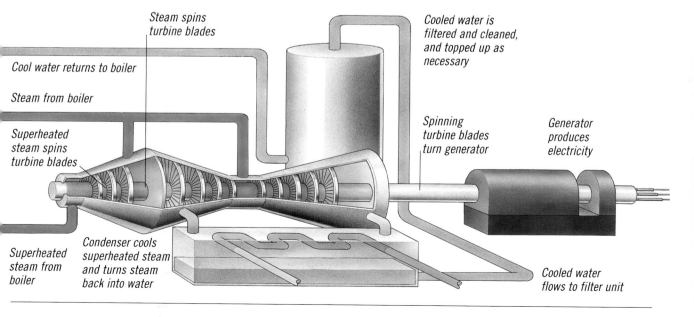

Steam spins turbine blades

Cooled water is filtered and cleaned, and topped up as necessary

Cool water returns to boiler

Steam from boiler

Superheated steam spins turbine blades

Spinning turbine blades turn generator

Generator produces electricity

Superheated steam from boiler

Condenser cools superheated steam and turns steam back into water

Cooled water flows to filter unit

Forces and motion

FORCES PUSH, PULL, PRESS and move things. Forces have size or strength – and also direction. A force always acts on an object in a particular direction. If the object is free to move, the force makes it move and speed up, or accelerate, in the direction of the force. When something cannot move, such as a nut in the jaws of a nutcracker, the force can change its shape or even break it apart altogether. When a force pushes against a surface, the result is pressure. The bigger the force, and the smaller the surface area, the higher the pressure.

Fun from forces
A child slides gently to the ground. The force of the child's weight acts straight downwards. But the angle of the slippery slide changes this force into two parts, one acting down and another pushing the child sideways. The steeper the slide, the bigger the downwards part of the force, and faster you go!

Laws of motion
Kick a soccer ball, and you force it to move. Once going, the ball tries to carry on in the same direction at the same speed. But two forces act on it, to change both speed and direction. These are air resistance and gravity. Kicking a ball shows three of the most basic ideas in all of science – the laws of motion.

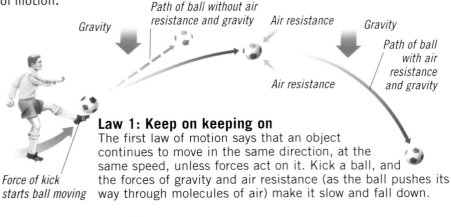

Gravity

Path of ball without air resistance and gravity

Air resistance

Gravity

Path of ball with air resistance and gravity

Air resistance

Force of kick starts ball moving

Law 1: Keep on keeping on
The first law of motion says that an object continues to move in the same direction, at the same speed, unless forces act on it. Kick a ball, and the forces of gravity and air resistance (as the ball pushes its way through molecules of air) make it slow and fall down.

Science discovery

Isaac Newton (1642–1727) was one of the most brilliant of all scientists. One of his greatest achievements was to work out the laws of motion and gravity. These affect everything in the Universe, from atoms and grains of sand, to the Earth, Moon, stars and galaxies in space. Newton also invented a new kind of mathematics, calculus.

Law 2: More means faster
The second law of motion says that the greater the force on an object, the faster the object picks up speed. That is, acceleration of an object is proportional to the force acting on it. So kick harder, and the ball goes faster.

Small force of a soft kick – ball rolls slowly

Large force of a hard kick – ball rolls faster

Roll balls together from opposite directions

Equal but opposite forces mean balls bounce back again

Law 3: Bouncing back
The third law of motion says that when an object hits another, the second object produces an equal force but in the opposite direction. In other words, for every action, there is an equal and opposite reaction. If two soccer balls hit each other, rolling at equal speeds in exactly opposite directions, they bounce apart and roll back the way they came.

See also: Gravity page 36, Friction page 42

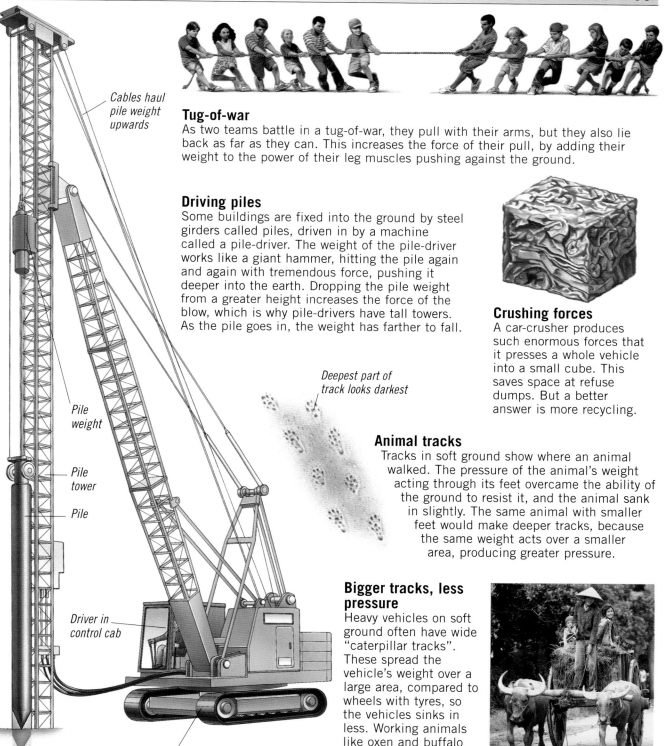

Cables haul
pile weight
upwards

Tug-of-war
As two teams battle in a tug-of-war, they pull with their arms, but they also lie back as far as they can. This increases the force of their pull, by adding their weight to the power of their leg muscles pushing against the ground.

Driving piles
Some buildings are fixed into the ground by steel girders called piles, driven in by a machine called a pile-driver. The weight of the pile-driver works like a giant hammer, hitting the pile again and again with tremendous force, pushing it deeper into the earth. Dropping the pile weight from a greater height increases the force of the blow, which is why pile-drivers have tall towers. As the pile goes in, the weight has farther to fall.

Crushing forces
A car-crusher produces such enormous forces that it presses a whole vehicle into a small cube. This saves space at refuse dumps. But a better answer is more recycling.

Deepest part of
track looks darkest

Animal tracks
Tracks in soft ground show where an animal walked. The pressure of the animal's weight acting through its feet overcame the ability of the ground to resist it, and the animal sank in slightly. The same animal with smaller feet would make deeper tracks, because the same weight acts over a smaller area, producing greater pressure.

Pile
weight

Pile
tower

Pile

Bigger tracks, less pressure
Heavy vehicles on soft ground often have wide "caterpillar tracks". These spread the vehicle's weight over a large area, compared to wheels with tyres, so the vehicles sinks in less. Working animals like oxen and buffalo have wide hooves, for the same reason.

Driver in
control cab

Pile rammed bit by
bit into ground

Caterpillar tracks prevent
sinking into soft ground

Gravity

WHEN YOU JUMP IN THE AIR, you quickly drop back to the ground. And however hard you throw a ball into the air, it always comes down again. The invisible force that pulls everything downwards on Earth is called gravity. But other objects have gravity, too. In fact, every object has gravity – the force called gravitational attraction.This attracts, or pulls, other objects. So a ball flying through the air pulls the Earth towards it, as well as the Earth pulling the ball.

But because the Earth has so much more mass than the ball, and so a much greater inertia (resistance to being moved), it is the ball that moves. Objects like stars are so massive, they have huge gravitational attraction. The Sun's gravity holds all the planets, including Earth, in orbit around it.

Earth and Moon
The Earth and Moon attract each other, but the Earth is much more massive. So the Earth stays almost still compared to the Moon, while the Moon goes around it.

Measuring gravity
Earth's gravity pulls objects down onto its surface. We can measure this force by the amount it stretches the spring in a spring balance. In everyday terms we call it "weight", and we measure it in kilograms. But in scientific terms, weight is a force and so it should be measured in units called newtons. Bigger objects with more mass (matter or atoms) are pulled more strongly to the Earth. In other words, they weigh more.

Leaning over
The world-famous Leaning Tower of Pisa, in Italy, was slowly being pulled over to one side by gravity. A tall thin object stands upright as long as its top is directly above its base. Then the force of gravity acts straight down through the object. The tower in Pisa was finished in about 1350 – but, unfortunately, it was built on soft ground. And on one side, the ground was slightly softer than the other. So the tower began to tilt to that side. In recent years, the foundations have been strengthened, and hopefully the Leaning Tower will not lean any further.

Skydiving to the max
Skydivers accelerate towards the ground until the force of gravity pulling them down is balanced by the force of air resistance pushing upwards against them. With these two forces in balance, the skydivers stop accelerating. Their final maximum speed of about 160 kilometres per hour is called their terminal velocity.

See also: Exploring space page 104

Gravity-powered spacecraft

The Cassini-Huygens spacecraft was launched in 1997 to the giant outer planet Saturn. But even the biggest rocket cannot launch a spacecraft straight to Saturn. So the craft uses the slingshot method (below).

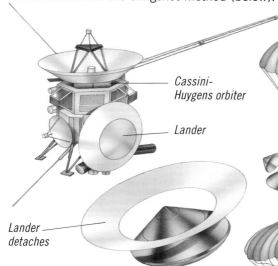

Cassini-Huygens orbiter

Lander

Lander detaches

Small parachute pulls off lander's cap

Rings of Saturn

The Cassini-Huygens probe landed on Saturn, with its spectacular rings, in the year 2004. The planet's gravity pulled the spacecraft faster and faster towards it. But the angle of the craft's approach meant that it went into orbit around Saturn. Then it released its lander probe. This sent radio signals to the orbiter part of the craft, which relayed them to Earth.

The slingshot method

The Cassini-Huygens craft was launched not towards Saturn, but at Venus. The gravity of Venus speeds it up until it swings around this planet like a slingshot and heads back to Earth. Earth's gravity gives it another boost, then it slingshots around the Sun, Venus again, and finally Jupiter, before arriving at Saturn.

Large parachute opens

Lander drifts down through dense gases of planet Saturn

SWINGING TIMES

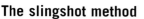

Pendulum clocks are driven by gravity. A weight hangs on a cord that is wound around a drum. Gravity pulls the weight down and so the weight tries to turn the drum. Each time the pendulum swings, it lets the drum rotate a small amount, using the escape mechanism. The pendulum also receives a tiny "kickback" from the drum, in return. This tiny kickback on each swing of the pendulum supplies enough energy to keep the pendulum swinging, and the clock ticking, for weeks or even months.

Drum

Cord

Weight

Pendulum

Lander's heat-shield faces downwards

Heat and cold

HEAT IS A FORM OF KINETIC ENERGY. It is the kinetic or movement energy of the atoms in a substance or object. When something is cold, its atoms vibrate, or move about quickly, very little. As the substance or object warms up, its atoms vibrate more and more. Temperature is not the same as heat. Heat is a form of energy. Temperature is a measure of how much heat something contains, or how much hotter or colder it is compared to something else. In normal temperature measurements, the "something else" is when water freezes into ice at 0°C, or boils into steam at 100°C. This is the Celsius (°C) temperature scale.

Hot shots
At high speeds, friction or rubbing with the air causes tremendous heat. So fast planes have outer coverings of metals such as titanium steel, which can withstand very high temperatures.

Measuring temperatures

Very accurate temperature measurements are made by a device called a thermocouple. It consists of two wires made from different metals joined together at their ends. The joined ends are called junctions. If the two junctions are at different temperatures, electricity flows through the wires. The size of the electric current depends on the difference in temperature – the greater it is, the more the current. If one junction is kept at a known temperature, for example 0°C, the temperature of the other junction can be worked out from the size of the electric current.

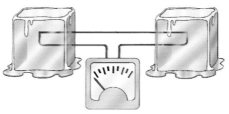

Both junctions at same temperature – no electricity

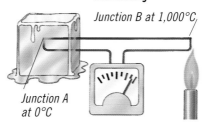

Junction B at 1,000°C

Junction A at 0°C

Junctions at different temperatures – electricity flows

Science discovery

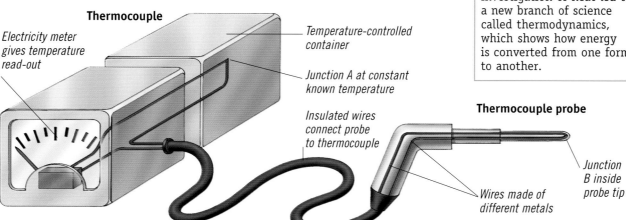

James Joule (1818–1889) was the first person to show that a certain amount of mechanical work, such as turning a handle, produces a certain quantity of heat. In other words, mechanical work and heat are two different forms of the same thing – energy. Joule's investigation of heat led to a new branch of science called thermodynamics, which shows how energy is converted from one form to another.

Thermocouple

Electricity meter gives temperature read-out

Temperature-controlled container

Junction A at constant known temperature

Insulated wires connect probe to thermocouple

Thermocouple probe

Junction B inside probe tip

Wires made of different metals

See also: Friction page 42, Flowing electricity page 52

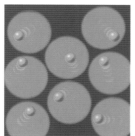

Very hot
In a very hot substance, the atoms or molecules move about a lot. The atoms do not simply swing to and fro, like tiny pendulums. They rush about in all directions, like a small ball (shown in green) bouncing around inside a much larger ball (shown in orange).

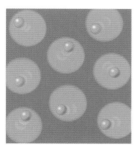

Cooler
When the amount of heat in a substance gets less, this means its atoms and molecules are moving less. We know that the quantity of heat is reduced because the substance feels cooler to the touch, and a thermometer shows that its temperature is lower.

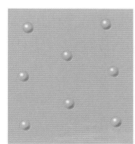

Very cold
A very cold substance has very little heat energy. This means that the atoms and molecules of the substance hardly move around at all. At the lowest possible temperature, which is called absolute zero, they completely cease to move and stay absolutely still.

Keeping out heat
Substances that allow heat energy to pass through them only very slowly are called thermal insulators. The layers of fibre-glass in the roof of a house are thermal insulation, to keep the warmth inside the house. Firefighting suits are made of a specially flexible thermal insulation material. They also have a smooth surface which reflects some of the heat energy. The surface reflects light rays too, which is why the suits are shiny.

Seeing heat
When we look at things, our eyes detect light rays. These are a form of electromagnetic radiation. As shown later in the book, heat travelling from one place to another is also a form of electromagnetic radiation, known as infra-red rays. Some satellite cameras detect infra-red rays rather than light rays. They take "heat pictures" such as the city shown above. Reds show the warmer parts, blues and black the colder ones.

THE RANGE OF TEMPERATURES
In daily life, we experience a very narrow range of temperatures. A cold day might be minus 10°C, while a hot day could be 32°C. The scientific scale for measuring temperature is called the Kelvin scale. Absolute zero is 0 K (minus 273.15°C). Water boils at 373.15 K (100°C).

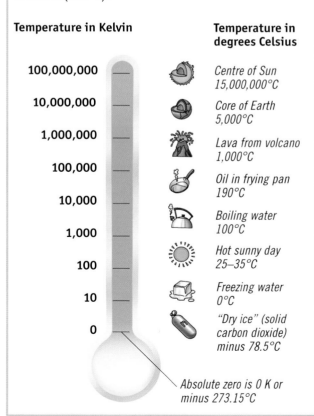

Temperature in Kelvin

Temperature in degrees Celsius

Temperature in Kelvin	Temperature in degrees Celsius
100,000,000	Centre of Sun 15,000,000°C
10,000,000	Core of Earth 5,000°C
1,000,000	Lava from volcano 1,000°C
100,000	Oil in frying pan 190°C
10,000	Boiling water 100°C
1,000	Hot sunny day 25–35°C
100	Freezing water 0°C
10	"Dry ice" (solid carbon dioxide) minus 78.5°C
0	Absolute zero is 0 K or minus 273.15°C

Simple machines

EVERY MECHANICAL DEVICE, even the most complicated giant earth-mover, is made from only four different types of simple machines. These are the lever, the inclined plane or ramp, the wheel and axle, and the pulley. The lever is a stiff beam or bar that pivots at a point called the fulcrum. If the fulcrum is closer to one end than the other, you can use a lever to lift a heavy weight more easily. The inclined plane (ramp or slope) is a machine too. It is usually easier to slide a heavy weight up a slope than to lift it straight up. Place two inclined planes back-to-back and they form a wedge, as in a knife blade, axe or chisel. A wedge wrapped around a rod, in the corkscrew-like shape called a helix, forms a screw. Screws are used to lift things and fasten them together.

Science discovery

The mathematician and inventor Archimedes (287–212 BC) of Ancient Greece discovered the principle of mechanical advantage that applies to levers and pulleys. These simple machines do not give something for nothing. A lever allows you to move a heavy weight with less effort than by lifting it directly – but the weight does not move very far. In the end, moving the weight the same distance, directly or with a lever, uses the same total amount of energy.

Building the pyramids

The pyramids were built in ancient Egypt about 4,500 years ago, from thousands of blocks of stone – some weighing many tonnes. These may have been levered into place, or dragged up a slope built beside the pyramid, or rolled up on logs. No one really knows.

Levers at work

The arms of a mechanical digger are made from a series of levers linked together. The arms are moved by oil pumped at very high pressure through pipes, or hoses, into a cylinder. The pressure of the oil pushes a piston along the cylinder and this provides the force, or effort, to move the arm. Cylinders and pistons used in this way are called hydraulic rams.

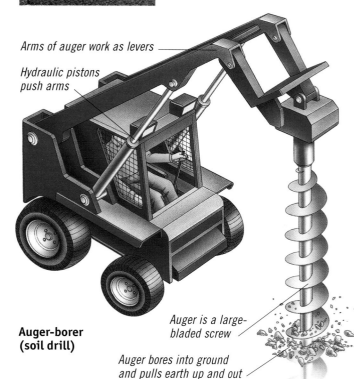

Arms of auger work as levers

Hydraulic pistons push arms

Auger-borer (soil drill)

Auger is a large-bladed screw

Auger bores into ground and pulls earth up and out

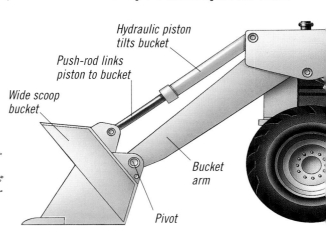

Hydraulic piston tilts bucket

Push-rod links piston to bucket

Wide scoop bucket

Bucket arm

Pivot

See also: Solids, liquids and gases page 16

DIFFERENT TYPES OF LEVERS

There are three different ways of arranging a lever's effort or moving force, its fulcrum or pivoting point, and its load – the object to be moved or pressed. These different ways are called the three orders of levers. The closer the fulcrum to the load, the easier it is to move the load. But you do not gain any overall advantage, since the load moves less distance.

First order lever

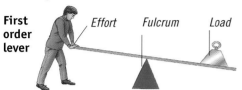

In the first order lever, the effort and load are at either end with the fulcrum in the middle, like a see-saw or crowbar. Two such levers sharing the same fulcrum form a pair of scissors or pliers.

Second order lever

In the second order lever, the effort is in the middle, with the fulcrum and load at each end. A mechanical digger's arm uses this arrangement.

Third order lever

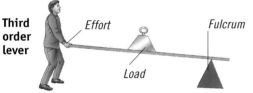

In the third order lever, the load is in the middle, between the fulcrum and effort, as in a wheelbarrow or a pair of nutcrackers.

Power of the wedge

A sculptor shapes a piece of stone using a mallet and chisel. The force of the mallet hitting the chisel is passed to the thin, sharp, wedge-shaped chisel blade. The mallet blow's large force acts on a tiny area at the blade tip, producing enormous pressure. The stone gives way and cracks apart.

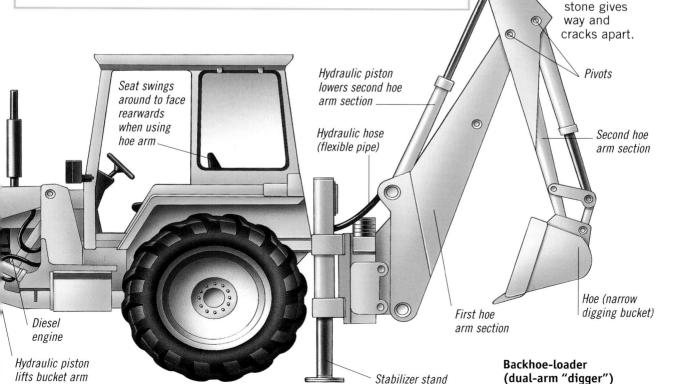

Seat swings around to face rearwards when using hoe arm

Hydraulic piston lowers second hoe arm section

Hydraulic hose (flexible pipe)

Pivots

Second hoe arm section

Diesel engine

Hydraulic piston lifts bucket arm

First hoe arm section

Hoe (narrow digging bucket)

Stabilizer stand

Backhoe-loader (dual-arm "digger")

Friction

FRICTION IS A FORCE that resists motion. It always acts in the opposite direction to the motion. Friction is caused by the lumps and bumps on two surfaces, rubbing and catching together as they slide across each other. Even the smoothest surface has these tiny lumps. Friction means that objects slow down and lose kinetic energy. This energy does not disappear, but changes into heat. Rub your hands and feel it! In machines, where parts are constantly sliding past each other, a thin film of oil or grease between the parts reduces rubbing, friction and wear. Using oil or grease to reduce friction is called lubrication.

Slow descent
A climber slides or abseils safely down a rope. The rope is wound in and out of steel hoops clipped to the climber's harness. Controlled friction between rope and hoops stops the climber falling too quickly.

BALL-BEARINGS

A bearing is part of a machine specially designed to reduce friction between moving parts. A ball-bearing reduces friction by replacing sliding with rolling. The two grooved collar-shaped parts of the bearing are called races. As the outer race stays still and the inner race rotates, the steel balls between them roll. Wheels often spin on their axles by means of ball-bearings.

Ball

Inner race

Outer race

Axle   Groove

Riding on air

A hovercraft glides over the water on a cushion of air. When a boat moves through water, the water pushes back against the boat and slows it down. This sort of resistance or friction is called drag (see opposite). In a hovercraft, air blows underneath the boat so fast that its pressure overcomes the boat's weight and lifts it above the surface. The hovercraft's rubber skirt helps to stop the air from escaping too fast and increases the height of the air cushion.

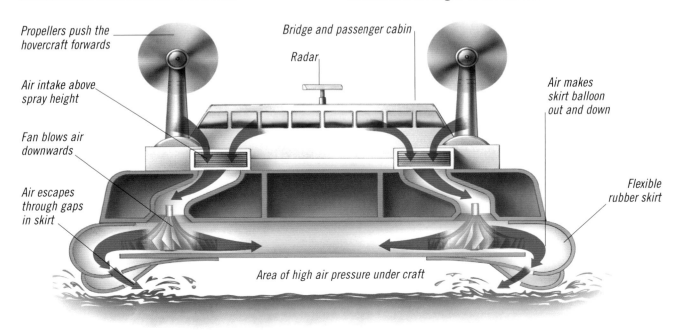

Propellers push the hovercraft forwards

Bridge and passenger cabin

Radar

Air intake above spray height

Air makes skirt balloon out and down

Fan blows air downwards

Air escapes through gaps in skirt

Flexible rubber skirt

Area of high air pressure under craft

See also: Water page 20, Forces and motion page 34

Vital friction

Friction is often called "the enemy of machines". Yet some machines rely on it, to work effectively. One example is the car brake. Friction between the brake discs and brake pads makes the wheel turn more slowly. Then friction between the wheel's rubber tyre and the road makes the car slow down.

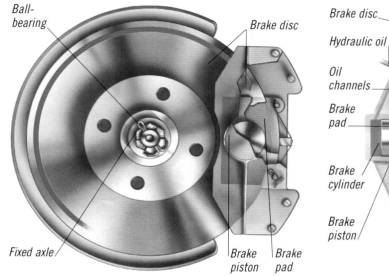

Ball-bearing

Brake disc

Fixed axle

Brake piston

Brake pad

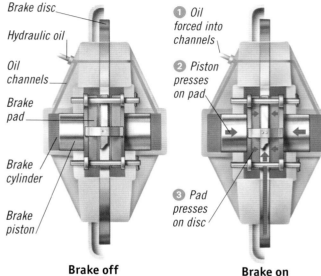

Brake disc

Hydraulic oil

Oil channels

Brake pad

Brake cylinder

Brake piston

1 Oil forced into channels

2 Piston presses on pad

3 Pad presses on disc

Brake off

Brake on

Disc brakes

When a car driver presses the brake pedal, oil is forced through pipes into cylinders on each side of a metal disc, the brake disc, attached to each road wheel. The oil pressure pushes pistons, which press roughed brake pads against the spinning disc. Friction between the disc and the pads slows the disc and wheel.

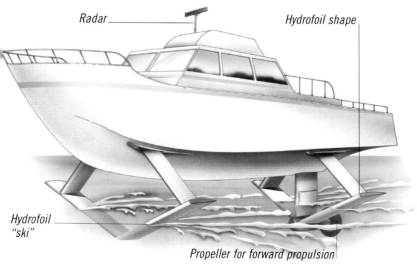

Radar

Hydrofoil shape

Hydrofoil "ski"

Propeller for forward propulsion

Flying through water

A hydrofoil is a boat with "skis". These have the same shape as an aircraft wing, more curved on the upper side than below, and work in the same way. As the boat moves forwards, water must go farther over the upper surface than the lower surface. So it moves faster. This creates lower pressure, and the hydrofoil is lifted upwards. At high speeds the boat rises right out of the water, greatly reducing the drag caused by friction.

Side view of hydrofoil

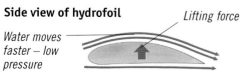

Lifting force

Water moves faster – low pressure

Energy for the world

MOST OF THE ENERGY USED all over the world comes from three sources – oil, coal and natural gas. These are called fossil fuels, because they are made of the rotted, semi-fossilized remains of living things from millions of years ago. Another common energy source is biomass – recently living material or products, such as wood or animal dung. In some parts of the world, biomass in the form of firewood is the only source of energy. Nuclear power is important in some countries, although it brings the problems of nuclear accidents and nuclear waste. Countries with high mountains and plenty of rain can generate electricity from the energy of flowing water. This is hydroelectric power.

Wind energy
Wind, water and muscle power were the main sources of energy for machines, until the steam engine was developed from the 17th century. The traditional windmill works by swivelling its sails into the wind so that they rotate with maximum force. The sails turn an axle that operates machinery inside the mill, such as millstones to grind corn.

Hydro-energy
A hydroelectric power station makes electricity from moving water. The water flows through pipes containing turbines, which spin around and turn generators. As the water pressure pushing against the turbine blades increases, the blades spin more powerfully, and generate more electricity. So, to increase the water pressure, and also to ensure a plentiful year-round supply of water, a dam is built across a river valley. Water piles up behind the dam, filling the valley and forming a lake.

Energy demand
Power stations feed their electricity into a grid or distribution network.

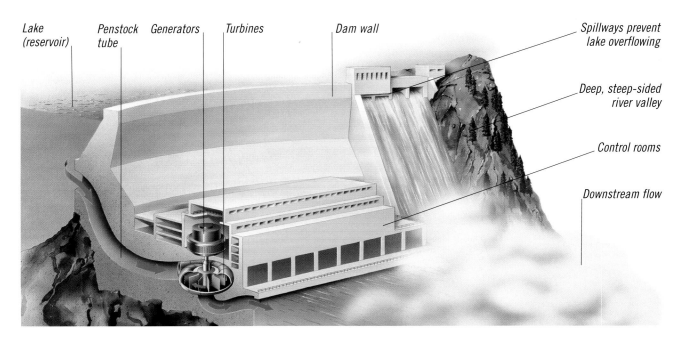

Lake (reservoir) Penstock tube Generators Turbines Dam wall Spillways prevent lake overflowing

Deep, steep-sided river valley

Control rooms

Downstream flow

See also: Water page 20, Converting energy page 32, Earth in trouble page 98

Science discovery
Marie Curie (1867–1934) taught herself science by reading books. When she heard about the discovery that uranium produced strange rays, she began to test other substances to see if they also produced such rays. Her word "radioactivity" describes the energies given off by such materials. Curie discovered two new radioactive elements, radium and polonium. Her work helped other scientists to develop nuclear power.

Using fossil energy
We are using up fossil fuels millions of times faster than they can be formed. At the present rates of use, known reserves of oil will run out in 100–200 years, and coal in 300–400 years. Also, mining coal which is at or near the surface, open-cast mining, scars the landscape.

WAVE ENERGY
Waves and tides carry a great deal of energy, which can be converted into electricity. A machine called a duck bobs up and down as waves wash past it. The rocking movement drives a generator, or pumps liquid or gas to spin a turbine that turns the generator. Another wave generator design is the oscillating water column. This is a tall chamber with one end under the water. Waves rise and fall inside the chamber and force the air in it through a turbine at the top. To harness the energy of tides, a dam-like barrier or barrage is built across the mouth of an inlet or bay. The tidal flow spins turbines inside the barrage.

Rocking "duck"

Each "duck" has its own shaft

Tilting shafts connected to generator

Sustainable and renewable energy
Our favourite form of energy is electricity. It can be transported huge distances along wires, and converted into movement, light, heat, sound and other useful forms. But our main sources of energy to make electricity – fossil fuels – will not last for ever. They are not sustainable or renewable, and they cause great pollution. So scientists are developing sustainable or renewable energy sources, which will not run out and which should cause less pollution. They include winds, waves, tides, sunlight, flowing water (hydro-energy) and hot rocks deep underground (geothermal energy). Aerogenerators or wind turbines are modern versions of windmills, making electricity from the energy in moving air.

Many wind turbines form a wind farm or park

3

Electricity and Magnetism

Electricity is a type of energy based on the movement of bits of atoms, called electrons. Magnetism is a mysterious and invisible force that can push or pull. Electricity produces magnetism, and magnetism produces electricity. Together they are the basis of innumerable machines, from motors to computers.

Electrical energy

ELECTRICITY IS AN INVISIBLE form of energy. It is based on the tiny charged particles inside atoms. In an atom's nucleus, particles called protons have a positive charge. Whizzing around the atom's nucleus are electrons, which have a negative charge. Normally, the positive and negative charges balance. If they become unbalanced, an electrical force is produced. This may stay in one place, as static electricity, or move from place to place, as a flowing current. Electricity is so useful to us because it can flow along wires to wherever we need it, and be changed into other forms of energy such as light, heat and movement.

Danger! Electricity!
Electrical energy can be very dangerous. An electric shock from a mains socket, which has a voltage of about 110 or 220 volts, can easily kill a person. The high-voltage (high-tension) electricity carried by cables on pylons is hundreds of thousands of volts. It can "jump" several metres through the air. So stay well clear!

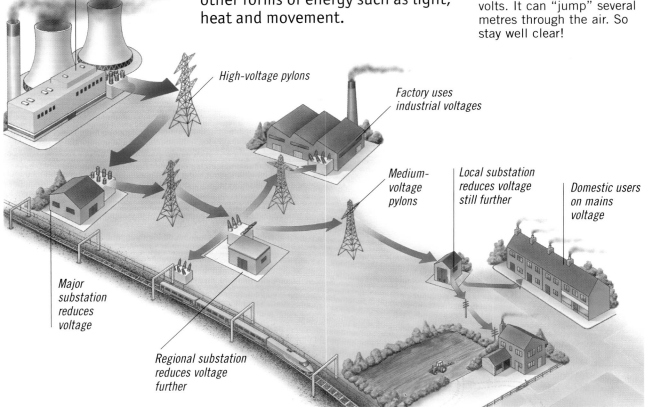

Power station with cooling towers

High-voltage pylons

Factory uses industrial voltages

Medium-voltage pylons

Local substation reduces voltage still further

Domestic users on mains voltage

Major substation reduces voltage

Regional substation reduces voltage further

The electricity network
Power stations turn the energy of movement into electrical energy which is medium strength, or mid-voltage. This is changed into more powerful, high-voltage electricity and sent along large cables or wires, high on pylons or buried underground. This network of cables and wires is called the electricity distribution grid. The electricity is changed back into lower-power forms, industrial and mains voltage, for use in factories, farms, offices and homes.

See also: Static electricity page 50, Flowing electricity page 52

Electricity in atoms

Everything is made up of trillions of incredibly tiny particles, called atoms. An atom has a central nucleus containing protons, each with a positive charge, and neutrons, each with no charge, or neutral. Going around the nucleus in empty space are much smaller particles, called electrons, each with a negative charge. When atoms or substances gain or lose electrons, they become electrically charged. Gaining electrons makes them negative. Losing electrons makes them positive.

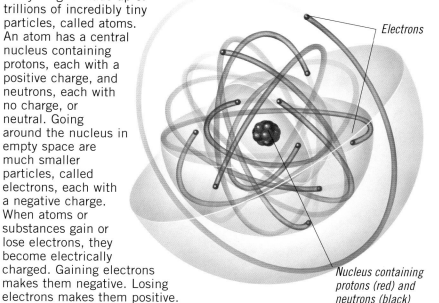

Electrons

Nucleus containing protons (red) and neutrons (black)

Science discovery

Benjamin Franklin (1706–1790) was one of the first people to study electricity in detail. In 1752, he flew a kite fitted with a metal key into a thundercloud. Sparks flew off the key, showing that lightning was a form of electricity. Franklin said that electricity consisted of two states of a mysterious fluid, an idea which is no longer believed.

Electricity at work

If there was a power cut in this city, people would have to manage without most of their lighting and heating, and the machines that make their lives so much easier. Daily routine would grind to a halt and the only sources of energy would be batteries, candles, wood, coal or gas. Yet people managed without electrical devices for thousands of years, and still do in many parts of the world. It is only in the last century or so that electricity has been put to work. One of its great advantages is that it is available at the flick of a switch.

SENSING ELECTRICITY

Sharks have a special sense which allows them to detect weak electrical signals. These are given off naturally by the muscles of their prey and travel well in water. A shark uses tiny sensory pits in the skin of the snout, called ampullae of Lorenzini, to detect the electricity. Other water-living animals can also detect electricity, including elephant-snout fish and squid. Electric eels, electric rays and electric catfish can also make powerful bursts of electricity to stun their prey.

Static electricity

YOU SHUFFLE ACROSS a carpet, touch a metal doorknob – zap! You feel a tiny electric shock as a spark jumps from you to the metal. This sort of electricity is called static electricity. It can make your hair stand on end, attract dust to the television set or stick a balloon to a wall. Static electricity builds up when two different non-metal materials rub together, as shown opposite. It can pull things together or push them apart, because opposite charges attract and like charges repel. Static can be destructive, as in a lightning strike, or useful, as in photocopiers, paint-sprayers and air-ionizers.

Lightning spark
Lightning is a way of releasing the electrical energy that builds up inside thunderclouds. It is a giant spark or discharge of static.

Using static

Photocopiers work using static electricity and the attraction of unlike charges. A rotating drum, coated with a material which allows electricity to flow when light shines on it, is positively charged with static electricity. Light from the white areas of the item to be copied shines on the drum and the charge flows away. The black areas keep their positive charge, and attract a negatively charged powder, the toner, which is then transferred to the paper.

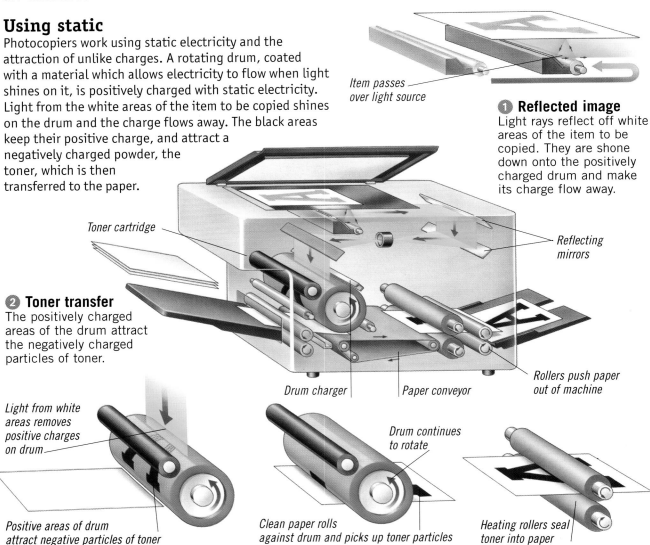

Item passes over light source

❶ Reflected image
Light rays reflect off white areas of the item to be copied. They are shone down onto the positively charged drum and make its charge flow away.

Toner cartridge

Reflecting mirrors

❷ Toner transfer
The positively charged areas of the drum attract the negatively charged particles of toner.

Drum charger *Paper conveyor*

Rollers push paper out of machine

Light from white areas removes positive charges on drum

Drum continues to rotate

Positive areas of drum attract negative particles of toner

Clean paper rolls against drum and picks up toner particles

Heating rollers seal toner into paper

See also: Electrical energy page 48, Mysterious magnetism page 60

Gigantic charges

Scientific research equipment such as Van der Graaf generators can produce massive amounts of static charge, measuring billions of volts. These charges are passed through substances and materials to study the effects, or given to atoms and other particles to make them travel at great speed.

Each copy requires the drum to be recharged

❸ Sealing toner

The tiny heat-sensitive particles of toner are "melted" into the paper by heating rollers. Meanwhile the drum is charged again, ready for the next copy.

Science discovery

The first photocopier was made by an American lawyer, Chester Carlson (1906–1968), in 1938. He called his process xerography, from the Greek words *xeros,* "dry" and *graphos,* "writing". At the time, writing was usually with ink and so wet at first. Those first copies took an hour or more to make. But they were valuable documents because they were exact replicas which could be used in law courts. Copying documents by hand might introduce mistakes.

SEPARATING CHARGE

Rubbing or friction makes electrons move. This gives one material a positive charge and the other a negative charge. The charges stay, or remain static, on the surfaces of the materials, until they have a pathway along which they can flow suddenly, or discharge. Static charge can pull things together or push them apart because (similar to magnets) opposite charges attract and like charges repel.

The two materials are brought near to each other. Each has billions of atoms. Each atom has a central nucleus (red) with one or more electrons (blue) going around it. The negative electron is kept near its positive nucleus by electrostatic forces, since unlike charges attract.

The energy of rubbing or friction gives electrons extra energy. This allows some of them to break free from their nuclei and wander off on their own. It is known as "separating charge". Some electrons pass or transfer from one material to the other.

One material has gained extra electrons and so becomes negatively charged. The other has lost electrons and is positively charged. The charges stay on the surfaces of the materials. (In a metal, the charges would be able to spread and disperse into the object.)

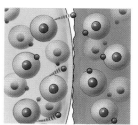

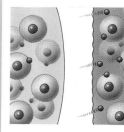

Charge-storers

Electronic circuits in hi-fi systems, televisions and computers have fingertip-sized devices called capacitors (shown here as light brown "buttons"). These are used to store static electrical charge. The charge can be released all at once at a certain moment, or in a steady series of steps.

Flowing electricity

WHEN YOU TURN ON A LIGHT, you are using the sort of electricity that flows along wires, like water flowing along pipes. This is called current electricity. It is usually made up of billions of electrons flowing along a wire or through an electrical component. These electrons do not move along a wire by themselves. They have to be pushed along by a difference in electrical state, called potential difference, produced by a battery or a power station. The power of an electric current is used to drive all kinds of machines in our homes, schools and workplaces.

Inside a wire

An electric current consists of billions of electrons, separated from their atoms, flowing along a wire. The electrons "hop" from one atom to the next, travelling in short bursts. Individual electrons move only fractions of a millimetre each second. But, like pushing a row of railway wagons, they have knock-on effects all along the wire. The result is that the effects of electricity travel at the speed of light, 300,000 kilometres per second.

Direct current, DC

In DC, all the electrons move in the same direction, all the time that the electricity flows. This type of current is produced by the batteries in torches, cars and similar devices.

Electrons moving along

Each atom has a central nucleus (red) and an area where electrons orbit (blue)

Alternating current, AC

In AC, the direction of electron movement changes many times each second. The electrons move one way, then the other, and so on.

Science discovery
Engineer Nikola Tesla (1856–1943) supported the now-accepted use of alternating current for most practical applications. In 1888 he built his first induction motor, which is the type of motor used in many domestic machines and appliances. He also invented a type of transformer, the Tesla coil, which produces enormous voltages and is used in radio technology.

Plastic covering or insulation stops electrons escaping from wire

Flow reverses

Flow reverses again

See also: Electrical energy page 48, Electricity from chemicals page 54

Electrons have knock-on effects along the whole wire

Keeping electricity in
Electricity passes or flows easily through some materials, mainly the metals that form wires. But it is stopped by other materials, such as plastic. So most wires and cables have plastic coatings, called electrical insulation.

Electrical cables
Electrical power cables are held above ground on pylons or towers, and buried underground in pipes or conduits. They can even be trailed down onto the sea bed by specialized cable-laying ships (above), linking one country with another hundreds of kilometres away. Similar cables are laid to carry telephone messages and electronic communications. But undersea earthquakes or fast-flowing currents of material on the sea bed, called turbidity currents, can snap these cables.

ELECTRICITY IN THE BODY
There are tiny electrical currents and pulses passing naturally through the body all the time. Some are nerve signals, moving around the brain, from the sense organs such as the eyes to the brain, and from the brain out to the muscles. A muscle also makes electrical pulses when it contracts to cause movement. The faint electrical pulses from the brain can be detected on the skin by sensors, strengthened and displayed on a screen or paper chart. The machine that does this is an EEG, electro-encephalograph.

Having an EEG is entirely painless. Sensors stuck on the skin of the head detect faint electrical signals coming naturally and continuously from the brain. The patterns of the signals show if the brain is healthy or if there could be a problem.

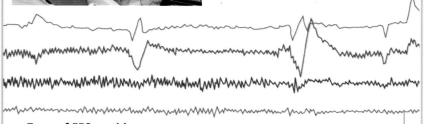

Trace of EEG machine showing "brain waves"

Jagged lines indicate electrical nerve signals

ELECTRICAL LETTERS
Electrical engineers and circuit designers use a variety of letters and symbols to describe the different features of electricity, such as its strength or quantity.

A   Amperes (amps), the unit for measuring amount or quantity of electric current.

AC   Alternating current, when the current's direction switches rapidly to and fro.

C   The amount of electrical charge that can be stored, in coulombs.

DC   Direct current, when the current's direction stays the same.

EMF   Electromotive force, the pushing strength of electricity measured in volts.

F   The amount of electrical capacitance, measured in farads.

HZ   The measure of how fast something happens (such as a.c.) in Hertz.

J   The amount of energy or work, including electricity, measured in joules.

KWH   Kilowatt-hour, how many thousand watts of power are made or used per hour.

P.D.   Potential difference, the pushing strength of electricity measured in volts.

V   Volt, the standard unit for measuring the pushing strength of electricity.

W   Watt, a standard unit of power, including electrical power.

Ω   Ohm, a measure of how much a substance resists electricity passing.

Electricity from chemicals

THE SIMPLEST UNIT for making electricity is called a cell. It makes electricity from chemical reactions and works like a pump to push electrons along wires. A battery has two or more cells and some types, such as car batteries, are rows or "batteries" of single cells, hence our common name "battery" for single and multiple cells. In a primary cell, as electricity is produced, the chemicals are slowly used up. Eventually, the chemicals run out and the battery cannot make electricity any more. In a secondary cell, the chemicals can be replenished or reformed by recharging the cell with electricity.

Electric animal
Muscles produce tiny electrical signals as they work. In the electric eel, these muscles form large blocks along the body. They produce powerful surges of electricity, hundreds of volts, like a "living battery".

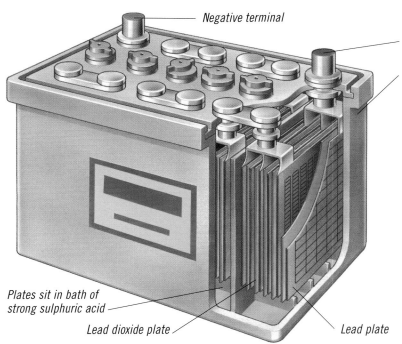

Negative terminal

Positive terminal

Acid-proof casing

Plates sit in bath of strong sulphuric acid

Lead dioxide plate

Lead plate

Car batteries

Also called an accumulator, a vehicle, batteries can be recharged. The chemical reaction which has taken place to make electricity can be reversed by putting electricity back in, so the battery can be used again. In a vehicle the recharging is carried out by an alternator, which is driven by the engine. Most car batteries have six linked cells, each with an output of about two volts. Each cell consists of lead plates, lead dioxide plates and sulphuric acid. Electricity is produced in the reactions between the plates and the sulphuric acid.

Substances such as acids dissolve in water to form charged particles, ions – positive cations (red) and negative anions (blue). In a cell, these form the electrolyte. When other materials, such as metal rods, are put in the electrolyte, they act as electrodes. They attract opposite-charged ions and cause an electric current to flow.

HOW A CELL WORKS

Positive ion Negative ion

The electrolyte consists of charge particles called ions, positive and negative.

Anode Cathode

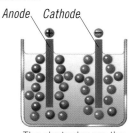

The electrodes are the positive anode and the negative cathode.

Electrons flow

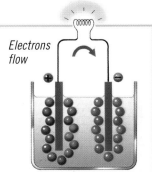

Opposite electrical charges attract and electrons move, making the current.

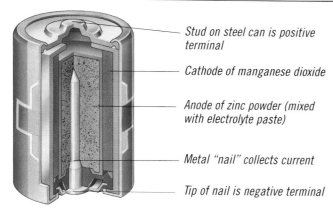

- Stud on steel can is positive terminal
- Cathode of manganese dioxide
- Anode of zinc powder (mixed with electrolyte paste)
- Metal "nail" collects current
- Tip of nail is negative terminal

Dry cell
"Dry" cells contain an electrolyte paste, rather than the liquid electrolyte in a vehicle battery. The long-life or alkaline dry cell has a combined anode (positive terminal) and electrolyte of powdered zinc in a paste.

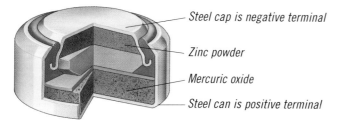

- Steel cap is negative terminal
- Zinc powder
- Mercuric oxide
- Steel can is positive terminal

Mercury-zinc "button" cell
This button-sized cell is used in watches, cameras, calculators, hearing aids and similar small devices. The anode is zinc powder and the cathode is mercuric oxide. Most button cells produce about 1.4 volts.

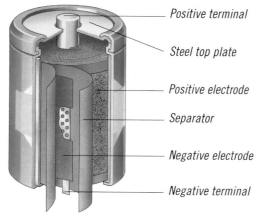

- Positive terminal
- Steel top plate
- Positive electrode
- Separator
- Negative electrode
- Negative terminal

Rechargeable or NiCad dry cell
The secondary or rechargeable dry cell is based on the metals nickel (Ni) and cadmium (Cd), hence the common name of "NiCad".

Science discovery
In 1800, Italian count Allessandro Volta (1745–1827) discovered that two different metals, separated by moist chemicals, could produce a flow of electric charge. This was the first electric cell. Volta piled the cells together on top of each other to make the first true battery, called the Voltaic pile. When he touched a wire from the top of the pile to a wire at the bottom, he got sparks of electricity.

This was the first time that a reliable supply of constantly flowing electrical current had become available. It began a whole new area of science, and sparked off a vast range of new inventions.

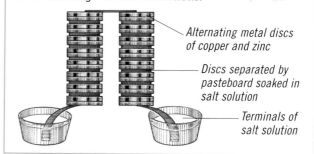

- Alternating metal discs of copper and zinc
- Discs separated by pasteboard soaked in salt solution
- Terminals of salt solution

HEART PACEMAKERS
Sometimes the tiny electrical pulses that make the heart beat naturally do not work properly. An artificial electrical pacemaker stimulates the heart to beat regularly, usually at one beat per second. It is powered by batteries which last at least five years, and sometimes up to 12 years. The artificial pacemaker detects when the heart is not producing its own electrical impulses and fills in the gaps.

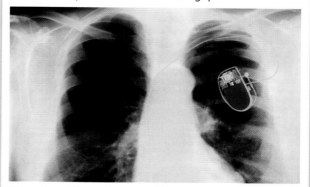

This coloured X-ray shows an artificial cardiac (heart) pacemaker, blue, implanted under the skin at the front of the chest. The heart is just below it, under the ribs.

Electrical circuits

IN SOME MATERIALS, called conductors, the electrons can easily leave their atoms and become free to move. This allows electricity to flow through them with little trouble. In other materials, called insulators, the electrons are held tightly in their atoms. This stops electricity flowing easily. The pathway that an electric current takes as it flows along is called a circuit. The current will only flow if the pathway is unbroken – a complete circuit. If there is a gap in a circuit, with air or another insulator in the way, electricity cannot flow. A switch is a device that makes or removes a gap in a circuit. This allows us to turn the electric current on and off.

Spur cable to water heater

Circuits at home

Electricity comes into a house through wires that go into a consumer unit, sometimes called the "fuse box". Then the wires divide into several branches or circuits called ring mains, some for the lighting and some for the power points in the wall sockets. One ring main consists of a cable that runs around the house, to all the power points one by one, and then back to the consumer unit. This allows electricity to reach a wall socket by flowing both ways around the ring, along the cables. This helps to share out the electricity demand around two routes, and avoids the problem of overload.

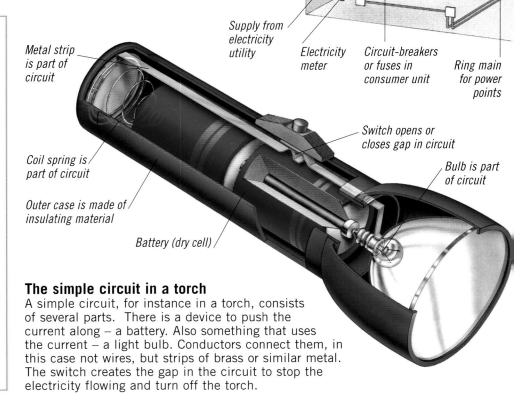

Supply from electricity utility

Electricity meter

Circuit-breakers or fuses in consumer unit

Ring main for power points

Science discovery

Georg Simon Ohm (1789–1854) showed that all conductors, even the best metals, resist the flow of electricity to an extent. The unit of electrical resistance is called the ohm in his honour. Ohm's law says that the current flow through a conductor, in amps, is proportional to the potential difference across it, in volts:

volts = amps x ohms

Metal strip is part of circuit

Coil spring is part of circuit

Outer case is made of insulating material

Battery (dry cell)

Switch opens or closes gap in circuit

Bulb is part of circuit

The simple circuit in a torch

A simple circuit, for instance in a torch, consists of several parts. There is a device to push the current along – a battery. Also something that uses the current – a light bulb. Conductors connect them, in this case not wires, but strips of brass or similar metal. The switch creates the gap in the circuit to stop the electricity flowing and turn off the torch.

See also: Electrical energy page 48, Flowing electricity page 52

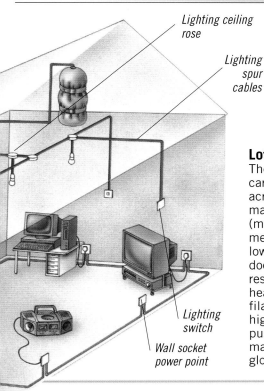

Lighting ceiling
rose

Lighting
spur
cables

Lighting
switch

Wall socket
power point

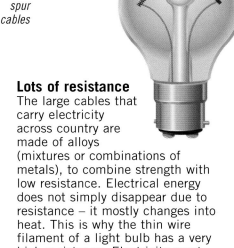

Lots of resistance

The large cables that carry electricity across country are made of alloys (mixtures or combinations of metals), to combine strength with low resistance. Electrical energy does not simply disappear due to resistance – it mostly changes into heat. This is why the thin wire filament of a light bulb has a very high resistance. Electricity must push hard to get through it. This makes the filament so hot that it glows with a bright white light.

CIRCUIT SYMBOLS

To save time and avoid confusion, circuit diagrams are drawn with small symbols that represent standard components. This is one of the many examples of the international scientific language of signs and symbols.

 Alternating current (AC)

 Ammeter (measures current)

 Electrical cell

 Fuse

 Relay

 Switch

 Transformer

 Voltmeter (measures p.d.)

 Resistor

 Variable resistor (rheostat)

 Coil (solenoid)

 Capacitor (stores charge)

 Preset capacitor

 Electrolytic capacitor

 Diode

 LED (light emitting diode)

 Bipolar transistor

Field effect transistor

TYPES OF CIRCUITS

There are many ways of connecting together various components and wires, to make circuits. In a series circuit, the components are joined one after the other. If one component is removed or fails, it breaks the circuit and nothing works. In a parallel circuit, each component has its own "mini-circuit". So if others fail, it still works.

Light bulb

Cell (battery)

Variable resistor

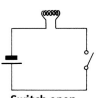

Switch open – no current flows

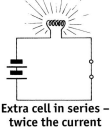

Extra cell in series – twice the current

Maximum variable resistance

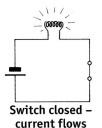

Switch closed – current flows

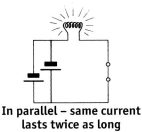

In parallel – same current lasts twice as long

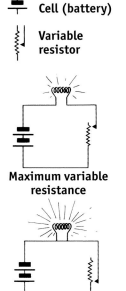

Minimum variable resistance

Electricity makes magnetism

ELECTRICITY IS CLOSELY RELATED to an invisible natural force called magnetism (which is described in more detail on the following pages). In fact, electricity and magnetism are two aspects of the same force, which modern science views as one of the four fundamental forces in the entire Universe – electromagnetism. When electricity flows through a conductor, such as a length of wire, it produces an invisible magnetic field around the wire. This is known as the electromagnetic effect. Magnets made in this way, by flowing electricity, are called electromagnets.

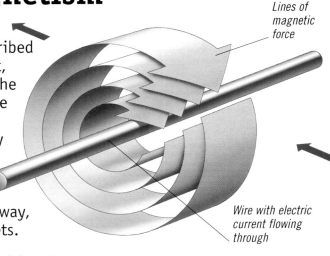

Lines of magnetic force

Wire with electric current flowing through

Lines of magnetic force

Magnetism is weaker farther from core

Plastic-coated wire with electric current flowing through

Magnetism concentrated at ends of core

Soft iron core

Invisible force
The magnetic field or force around an electricity-carrying wire goes in a circular direction, curling around the wire.

The electromagnet
A typical electromagnet consists of a coil of plastic-covered wire wrapped around an iron bar, which is known as the core. A coil of wire, or solenoid, produces a stronger magnetic field than a straight length of wire. The wire is connected to a source of electricity such as a battery. As soon as the electric current is switched on, the bar becomes a very powerful magnet. Switch off the electricity, and the magnetism disappears. Most electromagnets use soft iron for the core because this loses its magnetism as soon as the electricity is switched off. A hard steel core would keep its magnetism for a while.

Science discovery
In 1820, Danish scientist Hans Christian Oersted (1777–1851) noticed that a wire with an electric current passing through it worked like a magnet, making a needle on a nearby magnetic compass move. A compass needle is a tiny magnet and magnets can pull each other together or push apart. Oersted realized that the electric current was producing magnetism, and he was the first to discover the electromagnetic effect. Almost at once, many other scientists began to experiment with this effect.

See also: Flowing electricity page 52, Mysterious magnetism page 60

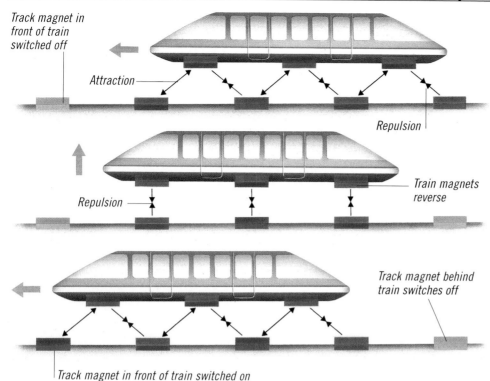

Track magnet in front of train switched off

Attraction

Repulsion

Repulsion

Train magnets reverse

Track magnet behind train switches off

Track magnet in front of train switched on

❶ Along
Electromagnets in the train and track produce pulling (attraction) and pushing (repulsion) forces that propel the train forwards.

❷ Up
The electromagnets in the train reverse their magnetic field for a split second, to produce strong repulsion forces and keep the train up.

❸ Along
The train electromagnets reverse their magnetism again, to propel the train forwards, and so on, many times each second.

Magnetic trains
Electromagnets are used instead of wheels on some trains. The train "floats" a few centimetres above the track, pushed upwards by a magnetic force produced by electromagnets. This type of train is called a maglev, meaning magnetic levitation. There have been many versions of maglev trains. However, most of them suffer from practical problems, such as the cost of laying and maintaining the specialized electromagnet-containing track.

Sorting metals
Powerful electromagnets are used in scrapyards to pick out and move certain objects from piles of mixed rubbish. Magnets attract the metal iron, and so steel (which is mostly iron), also nickel and cobalt. This electromagnet is attached to a crane.

Quiet and fast
A maglev train is quiet and fast. There is no noise from the wheels because no part of the train touches the track. Also, the train is not held back by friction with the track. But the maglev system uses large amounts of electricity and relies on complicated switching circuits. However, some maglev projects in progress today may help to make this type of transport more common.

Mysterious magnetism

HOLD A MAGNET near a refrigerator door. You can feel it being pulled towards the door. If you let go, the magnet "sticks" to the door. Yet it does not stick to a plastic beaker, a glass window or a piece of wood. The invisible force of magnetism remains mysterious, even though people have known about it for more than 2,000 years. Magnetism seems to be something to do with groups of atoms, called domains. In non-magnetic materials, the domains point in all directions and cancel each other out. In magnetic materials, all the domains point in one direction and their magnetic forces add up. Magnets attract mainly ferrous materials – those containing iron.

Lines of magnetic force are closest and so magnetism is strongest at the poles

Magnetic fields

Every magnet is surrounded by an invisible magnetic field, which is the space in which the force of its magnetism works. A pattern of imaginary lines provides a picture of this magnetic field. These lines of force show that the magnetic field is strong closest to the magnet but becomes weaker farther away. The power of a magnet is strongest at two points, called the poles, which are usually near the ends of a bar-shaped magnet. There are two poles, called the north and south poles. They are named after the poles of the Earth, to which they are attracted. Unlike poles attract. Like poles repel.

FINDING THE WAY

A compass needle points to the magnetic north pole and magnetic south pole of the Earth. This is because the compass needle is a small, thin magnet and the Earth is a giant magnet. So the needle lines up with the Earth's magnetic field. The needle in a compass is balanced on a fine point so that it can turn easily. The magnetic north pole is about 1,600 kilometres away from the true North Pole. The magnetic south pole is about 2,400 kilometres away from the true South Pole. The Earth's magnetic poles move a few centimetres each year and the strength of the Earth's magnetism changes slowly over long periods of time.

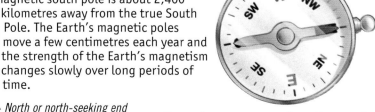

Compass needle points north

North or north-seeking end of compass needle

Base of compass turned to align north on dial with north-pointing needle

See also: Electricity makes magnetism page 58

■ **South pole**

■ **North pole**

Lines of magnetic force become farther apart, or weaker, farther from the magnet

Lines of magnetic force are parallel to the long bar of the magnet

Magnetic animals
Ships and boats use magnetic compasses to help them navigate across the featureless ocean. Certain animals, such as whales, dolphins and sea turtles, and birds like pigeons, swallows, geese and storks, also seem to use the Earth's magnetic field to help them find their direction and route on long journeys. Scientists are not sure how these animals detect the magnetism. It could be connected with tiny particles of iron-containing minerals inside or near the brain, which may form a "living compass".

Science discovery
Charles Coulomb (1736–1806) was an army engineer who turned to the physical sciences in 1791. He studied the attraction and repulsion forces produced by magnets and by objects with electrostatic charge. He invented a torsion balance, based on twisting a piece of stiff wire, that could measure tiny forces accurately. He used this to develop his law, which showed that magnetic forces fade rapidly, by the square of the distance between the magnetic objects.

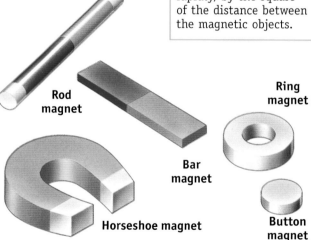

Rod magnet

Ring magnet

Bar magnet

Horseshoe magnet

Button magnet

Magnet shapes
Magnets can be made in different shapes. Bar magnets are long and narrow, while horseshoe magnets are curved like the metal shoes on a horse's hooves. Magnets can also be made in rings or thin cylinders, like pencils. A ring magnet can have one pole around the inside of the ring and the other on the outside.

Lines of magnetic force curve around to pole of magnet

Communications

MODERN COMMUNICATIONS DEVICES give almost instant access to almost any information, almost anywhere in the world. Most work using electricity and magnetism, and some use light too. Telephones and televisions rely on converting sounds or pictures into electrical signals, which are sent long distances through wires at high speed – the speed of light, 300,000 kilometres per second. Information can also be converted from electrical signals into pulses of electromagnetic waves – laser light – and sent along fibre-optic cables. Or it is changed into radio waves and sent to local networks, or up to satellites in space and then back down to Earth again. The light or radio signals have to be converted into electrical signals before they can be turned back into sounds or pictures again.

The electronic age
In the last 170 years, electrical information has revolutionized the way we communicate. Long-distance or telecommunications networks can pass messages around the world in seconds. These amazing achievements all started with the electric telegraph, which developed into the modern telex system. The telephone network has now developed to carry pictures, computer data, electronic mail and many other forms of information.

Fibre-optics

An optical fibre is a rod of glass or similar transparent material, which is thinner than a hair and can flex or bend. It is contained in a protective sheath that also separates it from other optical fibres around it. The fibre carries information as coded flashes of laser light. Because these hit the inside of the surface of the rod at a very shallow angle, they bounce off or reflect back into the rod, by total internal reflection. This means the laser pulse zig-zags along the inside of the fibre, even if it is bent. The flashes carry information in digital form. As with electrical information, a flash or pulse is 1 in binary, and no flash or pulse (a gap) is 0. The digital information can represent numbers, letters, words, sounds and pictures. Thousands of optical fibres are bundled together in one casing as a fibre-optic cable.

Strong waterproof outer covering

Steel core gives entire cable strength against stretching or kinking

Fibre made of special glass

Laser light pulses inside fibre

Different colours or wavelengths of light carry different messages

Outer sheaths protect cable from knocks and kinks

Each fibre has a colour-coded protective casing

See also: Using light page 80

Science discovery

In the 1920s, Vladimir Zworykin (1889–1982) devised the iconoscope or television transmission tube, and the kinescope, or television receiver. These two inventions formed the first all-electronic television system and provided the trigger for the development of modern television. The modern television picture tube is basically Zworykin's kinescope. The first regular television broadcasts began in 1936 in London, England. Zworykin also helped to develop a colour television system and the electron microscope.

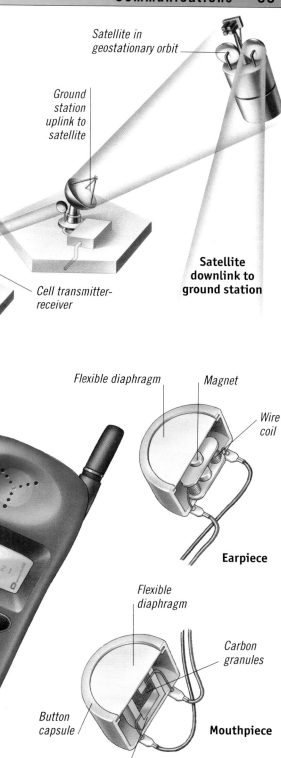

Satellite in geostatationary orbit

Ground station uplink to satellite

Satellite downlink to ground station

Cell transmitter-receiver

Telecom network

A mobile phone sends and receives messages by radio waves. The radio waves travel to and from a transceiver (transmitter/receiver) station which connects the calls into the standard telephone network. Countries are divided up into different areas, called cells, and each cell has its own transceiver station. In an area where a lot of people live, there are many small cells because there are likely to be many people using mobile phones. In sparsely populated areas, the cells are larger.

Network of cells

Flexible diaphragm

Magnet

Wire coil

Earpiece

Flexible diaphragm

Carbon granules

Mouthpiece

Inside a mobile phone

A "mobile" is a low-power radio transmitter-receiver. It has a mouthpiece to change sound waves into electrical signals (like a microphone), and an earpiece to change electrical signals into sound waves (like a loudspeaker). The transmitter-receiver only needs to send and pick up waves from the nearest cell tower, which is usually just a few kilometres away. However, hills or tall buildings may block the radio signals. Also, in areas where the cell towers are farther apart, the signals may be too weak to travel to and from the phone.

Button capsule

Metal contacts

4

Sound and Light

Some types of energy are in the form of up-and-down waves. They include sound and light – but the nature of their waves is very different. Sound is moving atoms and molecules. Light is combined electricity and magnetism. Both are sensed by the body, and are used to convey information.

About waves

SOUND AND LIGHT are both forms of energy. They are very different forms of energy – sound is made by something moving, while light is a mixture of electrical and magnetic energy. But sound and light are similar in that they both travel in regular up-and-down curved patterns, called waves. These are similar to ripples on a pond or the waves you make if you shake a rope up and down. In science, a wave is a travelling change, disturbance or fluctuation that passes energy from one place to another. Sound can travel only by moving particles of matter, such as the atoms or molecules that make up a substance. So sound cannot exist in, or travel through, the nothingness of a vacuum, such as space. Light, on the other hand, does not need matter or substance. It exists as tiny packets or parcels of energy called photons. These can travel through a substance such as air or water, and also through a vacuum.

Peak or crest (highest point) of first wave

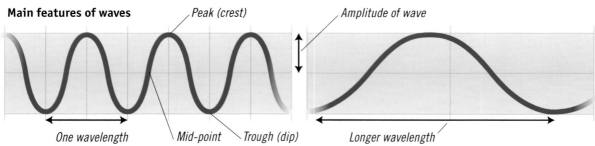

Main features of waves

Peak (crest)

One wavelength   *Mid-point*   *Trough (dip)*

Amplitude of wave

Longer wavelength

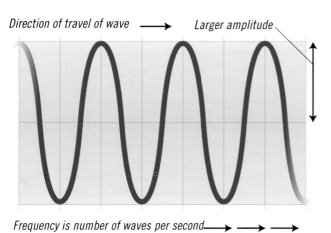

Direction of travel of wave ⟶   *Larger amplitude*

Frequency is number of waves per second ⟶ ⟶ ⟶

Features of waves

All waves have certain features. The highest part is the peak (crest). The lowest part is the trough (dip). The height of a wave, from its mid-point up to its peak, or from the mid-point down to its trough, is the amplitude. For sound, bigger amplitudes (taller waves) make louder sounds. For light, they make brighter lights. The number of waves passing a place or point in one second is called the frequency of the wave. The distance along one complete wave – for example, from one peak to the next – is the wavelength. For waves travelling at the same speed, the shorter the wavelength, the more waves pass a place during a given time. So shorter waves have higher frequencies.

See also: Sound waves page 68, Light page 74

Similar, but different

The watery ripples on a pond, after a stone is thrown in, help us to imagine the shape of sound and light waves. However, the sizes of these waves are very different. Light waves rise and fall several hundred million million times every second, and there are millions of peaks and troughs in one centimetre. Sound waves are much bigger. Each of the sound waves in a low hum is a metre or more long. Also, light waves travel a million times faster than sound waves.

Waves spread out, or emanate, from their central source

Science discovery

James Clerk Maxwell (1831–1879) used mathematics to explain the features of waves. He studied the links between electricity and magnetism. His calculations showed that electrical-magnetic waves travel at the speed of light. So he suggested a new idea for the time – that light itself was also electromagnetic waves. This is now accepted.

INVISIBLE AND INAUDIBLE

Our experience of sights and sounds is affected by the limits of our own sense organs – our eyes and ears. There are forms of light, such as infra-red and ultra-violet, which our eyes cannot detect. But the eyes of many animals can see them. Some animals can see well at light levels which are so low, we think it is completely dark. A cat may peer into the night, obviously watching intently. Yet we see only blackness. Also, there are sounds which are too quiet, or too low-pitched, or too high-pitched, for our ears to register. But dolphins, bats and many other animals can hear (and make) them. A dog or a horse may prick up its ears at a sound which is so faint, we hear nothing.

UV on flowers
Bees see lines called honey guides on flower petals. The lines show up only in ultra-violet (UV) light. They guide the bee to the honey in the centre of the flower.

IR in water
Goldfish see infra-red (IR) light, which is less filtered out by water, compared to normal light.

The common dolphin emits fast, high-pitched clicks and squeals

US at night
Bats such as the horseshoe bat send out very high-pitched (ultrasonic, US) squeaks through the nose and mouth. They detect the reflections or echoes with their large ears.

Sound waves

A SOUND WAVE starts with something moving. The something can be any state of matter – solid, liquid or gas. Usually, it is a solid. The object moves to and fro, or vibrates. It pushes and then pulls against the particles of the substance around it, which can also be any state of matter, but is usually air. The moving object squashes the molecules of air closer together, and then stretches them farther apart. These molecules push and then pull the ones next to them, and these do the same, and so on, passing on the wave of energy. So a sound wave is a series of invisible squashes and stretches that ripple through the air.

Musical sounds
All sound waves are made in the same way, by vibrating objects. Whether they are harsh and unpleasant, like the roar of traffic, or musical and pleasant, depends on how different sound waves are combined.

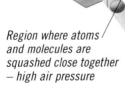

Sound source
(loudspeaker)

Sound wave

Atoms and
molecules of air

Region where atoms
and molecules are
squashed close together
– high air pressure

Region where atoms and
molecules are pulled farther
apart – low air pressure

Sound on the move

Sound travels through substances when the particles they are made of – atoms, or atoms joined together into molecules – move back and forth. Each atom or molecule hits another and then returns to its original position. The energy is passed on from one to the next, as though moving along links in a chain. But the atoms or molecules themselves only move short distances from their central positions. We picture sound as a wave, but really it is areas of particles closer together and farther apart, rippling outwards from the source. In air, these ripples are regions of high and low air pressure. As the particles collide, tiny amounts of energy are lost from the wave each time. So the wave gradually fades with distance.

See also: Light page 74

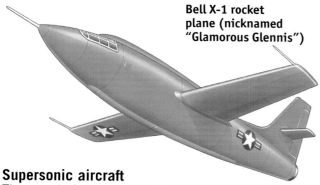

Bell X-1 rocket plane (nicknamed "Glamorous Glennis")

Supersonic aircraft

The speed of sound, or sonic speed, is called Mach 1. It varies with the pressure and temperature of the air, but is about 1,200 kilometres per hour. Something that travels faster than sound is known as supersonic. Twice the speed of sound is Mach 2, and so on. Some planes can reach Mach 3 or more. The first person to fly faster than the speed of sound was Captain Charles "Chuck" Yaeger in a rocket plane, the Bell X-1. It blasted through the sound barrier in 1947. Supersonic aircraft overtake their own sound, which spreads out behind them in a shock wave that we hear on the ground as a sonic boom.

Ocean sounds

Sound travels through water at about 1,430 metres per second – five times faster than it travels through air. Many water-living animals use sounds for communication. The deep or low-frequency calls of the great whales travel for hundreds of kilometres through the seas. Male humpback whales sing to attract females. Each individual has its own song and repeats it with small variations for hours on end. Mother great whales and their babies, or calves, also make clicks and squeals.

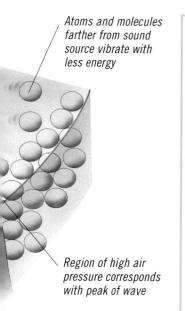

Atoms and molecules farther from sound source vibrate with less energy

Region of high air pressure corresponds with peak of wave

Region of normal air pressure corresponds with mid-point of wave

Region of low air pressure corresponds with trough of wave

THE DOPPLER EFFECT

Have you noticed how the noise of a speeding vehicle, like a motorcycle, car, train or plane, seems to be constant as it approaches you – then as it goes past, the noise drops or falls in pitch, to a lower note? As the vehicle moves towards you, it travels a small distance closer between sending out each sound wave. So for you, the sound waves are squashed closer together and make a high sound. As the vehicle passes, it now travels a small distance away between sending out each sound wave. So the sound waves are more stretched out, and make a lower sound, as shown on the next page.

Sound waves are farther apart, giving lower pitch behind

Sound waves are nearer together, giving higher pitch in front

Moving sound source

The Doppler effect is named after the Austrian scientist Christian Doppler, who first discovered it in 1842. It is especially noticeable with high-pitched sounds such as sirens. It happens with any form of waves, including light waves, when it is called "red shift".

High and low sounds

THE PITCH OF A SOUND means how low or high it is. In a music band, the bass drum's deep boom is low-pitched, while the triangle's shrill tinkle is high-pitched. Pitch depends on how many times the sound source moves to and fro, or vibrates, each second. This is the same as the frequency – how many sound waves are produced each second. The frequency of a wave is measured in units called Hertz, Hz. For example, the note of middle C, in the middle of a piano keyboard, has a frequency of 261 Hz. Frequency is related to wavelength, since higher frequencies have shorter waves. The length of a middle C sound wave is 126 centimetres.

What sounds can we hear?

We hear many sound frequencies, from the shrill notes of bird song to the deep growl of traffic. But, because of the way our ears work, we do not hear all of the sounds around us. Our ears pick up frequencies from about 20 to 20,000 Hz (Hertz, vibrations per second). We hear sounds below 80 Hz as low, deep booms, thuds or rumbles. Frequencies below about 30 Hz may not be heard clearly, but, if they are powerful enough, we can feel them as vibrations in the air and ground. Our ears are most sensitive in the range from 400 to 4,000 Hz. (Human speech tends to be around 300–1,000 Hz.) Sounds above about 5,000 Hz are extremely high-pitched squeaks, hisses and screeches. As people get older, their ears become less sensitive to high notes. So a young person can hear a bat's very high-pitched squeaks, while an older person cannot.

Science discovery

The unit of frequency for waves, Hertz, is named after physicist Heinrich Hertz (1857–1894). The unit is used for sound waves, and also for other waves, such as radio and light waves. In fact, Hertz worked mainly with radio waves, rather than sound. He was the first to make radio waves in a laboratory experiment. But he died before he could expand his work and make radio into a practical form of communication.

Animal ears

Compared to many animals, humans can hear a wide range of frequencies. However, some animals hear frequencies which are too high-pitched for our ears. These are called ultrasonic sounds.

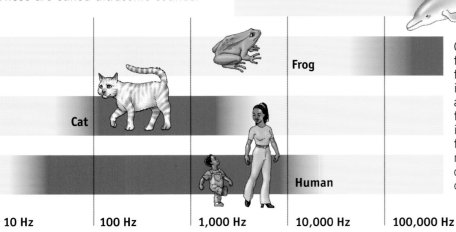

Bat

Dolphin

Frog

Cat

Human

| 10 Hz | 100 Hz | 1,000 Hz | 10,000 Hz | 100,000 Hz |

Other creatures detect frequencies which are too low for our ears. They are known as infrasonic sounds. Most animals hear the sound frequencies which are most important for their survival. The frog's hearing range is based mainly around the croaks of other frogs, which it needs to detect at breeding time.

See also: Solids, liquids and gases page 16, Sound waves page 68

Musical notation

We can hear sound waves, but not see them. Also sounds soon fade away in time. So we write or print a visual version of sounds and musical notes, known as musical notation. This helps people to remember the music and also preserves the music over time. The notation has symbols for the pitch (frequency), length (duration) and loudness of the sounds.

Crash cymbal
Ride cymbal
Hi-hat cymbals
Snare drum
Floor tom-tom
Bass drum
Mounted tom-tom
Hi-hat foot pedal

Musical instruments

Anything that can produce sounds of different timing or pitch is a musical instrument. The three main types of musical instrument produce their sounds in different ways. Stringed instruments, like the guitar and violin, are plucked or rubbed. Percussion instruments, such as drums, are tapped or hit. You blow a wind instrument, like a recorder or trombone.

Elephant sounds

About two-thirds of the noises that elephants make are too low for the human ear to detect. They are infrasonic sounds. They include more than 20 different types of rumbling calls, powerful enough to communicate with elephants more than 5 kilometres away.

Unwanted noise

Noises are generally unpleasant, unwanted jumbles of sound waves. They may be from loud music, machinery such as saws and drills, and vehicles, trains and planes. Noisy surroundings make it hard for people to think, relax or sleep. This can lead to stress or illness. Very loud or prolonged noise can damage hearing, as shown on the next page.

Sounds in solids, liquids and gases

In general, sounds travel farther and faster through solids than through liquids, and farther and faster through liquids than through gases such as air. This applies especially to low-pitched or low-frequency sounds. In a gas, the molecules are far apart, so much of the sound energy is lost in pushing the gas molecules about until they bump into other gas molecules. In a liquid or solid, the molecules are much closer together, so they bump into each other more easily as they vibrate with sound energy. This means the sound moves more quickly. So we sometimes feel the vibrations of a big sound source like a truck through the ground, before we hear it.

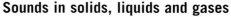

Loud and soft sounds

LOUD SOUNDS ARE LOUD because the atoms or molecules carrying them vibrate by large amounts, representing lots of energy. Soft or quiet sounds have much smaller vibrations. The loudness or volume of a sound is the strength of that sound as it reaches the ear. This is slightly different from the intensity of a sound, which is the amount of energy flowing along in the sound waves. Intensity depends on both pitch (frequency) and height (amplitude) of the sound wave. The loudness of a sound might be perceived as different from one person to another, but the intensity of the sound energy is the same for everyone.

Ear protection
People who work in noisy places, like textile factories or airports, or who use noisy machinery, protect their ears with ear-defenders. Continual higher-pitched sounds such as whines are most damaging to the ears.

Atomic explosion 200 dB

Blue whale grunting 170 dB

The decibel scale

The measurement scale which compares the intensities of sounds – which are similar to their loudness or volume – is called the decibel scale. Its units are decibels (dB), named after Alexander Graham Bell, who invented the telephone. A measure of 10 dB is the faintest sound that the human ear can detect, such as the rustling of dry leaves. Normal conversation measures about 60 decibels. Sounds become physically painful above about 130 dB. Even in the loudest sounds carried through air, the atoms and molecules of air do not move very much, only fractions of a millimetre.

Jet plane nearby 140 dB

Dangerously loud music 120 dB

Warning!
Warning signs show that loud noises might cause damage to the ear and loss of hearing, which could even be permanent.

Legal limit
In some regions, local regulations restrict sound levels in public places to 100, 90 or even 80 dB.

| 200 Decibels | 175 Decibels | 150 Decibels | 125 Decibels |

See also: Sound waves page 68

HOW MANY DECIBELS?

Some examples of decibel levels are shown in the chart below. Here are some more:
- 180 dB Rocket launch about 50 metres away
- 160 dB Rocket launch about 200 metres away
- 140 dB Huge machinery such as steelworks
- 110 dB Road drill (pneumatic jackhammer)
- 100 dB Nearby clap of thunder
- 80 dB Speeding train
- 20 dB Just audible whisper
- 10 dB Faint rustle of wind in long grass

ANIMAL EARS
Some animals, like rabbits and horses, have large ear flaps that they can tilt and swivel. They do this to locate the source of a sound. Humans cannot swivel their ears this well! But if you hear a sound, you can turn your head until the sound waves reach both of your ears at the same time and with the same volume. Then you are facing the source of the sound.

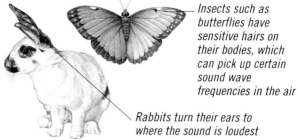

Insects such as butterflies have sensitive hairs on their bodies, which can pick up certain sound wave frequencies in the air

Rabbits turn their ears to where the sound is loudest

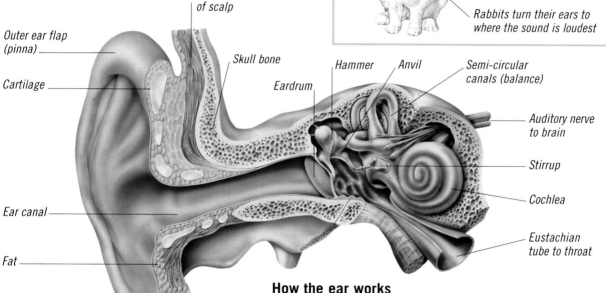

Skin and muscle of scalp · *Skull bone* · *Hammer* · *Anvil* · *Semi-circular canals (balance)* · *Eardrum* · *Auditory nerve to brain* · *Stirrup* · *Cochlea* · *Eustachian tube to throat* · *Outer ear flap (pinna)* · *Cartilage* · *Ear canal* · *Fat* · *Ear lobe*

How the ear works
The human ear has three main parts – the outer, middle and inner ear. The outer ear is like a funnel collecting sounds from the air. It leads to a tube, the ear canal, which ends in a flexible, circular eardrum. Sounds make the eardrum vibrate and this, in turn, makes three small bones in the middle ear vibrate too. The bones pass the sound vibrations to the cochlea in the inner ear, where they are changed into nerve signals that go to the brain.

Chainsaw 100 dB · **Loud conversation 70 dB** · **Soft conversation 50 dB** · **Bird song 30 dB** · **Ticking watch 10 dB**

100 Decibels | **75 Decibels** | **50 Decibels** | **25 Decibels**

Light

WE SEE LIGHT, and only light. We use light every day, in endless ways. But describing light is more difficult. It's a type of energy caused by a combination of electrical and magnetic fields. In some ways, light travels as waves, so it has typical wave features. For example, the colour of light depends on how long its waves are. However, in other ways, light seems to be a stream of tiny particles or packets of energy, called photons. Scientists have come to accept these two ways of understanding light. They call it the "wave-particle duality" of light. Nothing travels faster than light – it flashes along at almost 300,000 kilometres each second.

Invisible light

Light with waves which are shorter than the waves of violet light is called ultra-violet light, UV. Our eyes do not detect UV, so we cannot see it. But too much UV can cause sunburn and also damage our eyes.

Rainbow colours

A rainbow is caused by light from the Sun shining through raindrops. The raindrops separate out the colours in white light, so we can see them. The major colours in a rainbow are red, orange, yellow, green, blue, indigo and violet. They are always in the same order. These colours are called the spectrum. Each is light of a different wavelength. Red light has the longest waves, orange is slightly shorter, and so on. Violet has the shortest waves.

Colours of spectrum merge into each other

Clear and fuzzy

Some substances let most of the light pass straight through them. These clear materials, such as air, window glass or water, are called transparent. Other substances let some light through, but the waves are scattered and bounced around. So the view is fuzzy or blurred. These translucent substances include frosted glass, mist, net curtains and tracing paper. A substance that lets no light through is known as opaque.

Science discovery

One of the first scientists to study light in a scientific way was Alhazen (965–1038). At the time, most people believed that light came out of the eyes and shone onto objects, so that we could see them. Alhazen worked out the correct explanation – that light from a light source, such as the Sun or a candle, reflected off objects and went into the eye. He also studied coloured lights, mirrors and lenses. His work helped later scientists to develop the microscope, telescope and other optical, or light-based, devices. Sadly, for a person who helped to explain so much about light, lenses and how eyes work, there is no known portrait of Alhazen. So we do not know what he looked like.

An early compound microscope (one with more than one lens)

See also: About waves page 66

COLOURS AND FILTERS

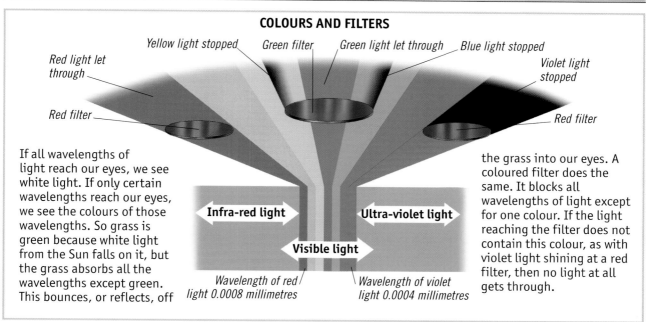

Red light let through

Yellow light stopped

Green filter

Green light let through

Blue light stopped

Violet light stopped

Red filter

Red filter

Infra-red light

Ultra-violet light

Visible light

Wavelength of red light 0.0008 millimetres

Wavelength of violet light 0.0004 millimetres

If all wavelengths of light reach our eyes, we see white light. If only certain wavelengths reach our eyes, we see the colours of those wavelengths. So grass is green because white light from the Sun falls on it, but the grass absorbs all the wavelengths except green. This bounces, or reflects, off the grass into our eyes. A coloured filter does the same. It blocks all wavelengths of light except for one colour. If the light reaching the filter does not contain this colour, as with violet light shining at a red filter, then no light at all gets through.

Mixing colours

Most colours of light can be made by mixing together just three colours – red, blue and green. These are called the primary colours of light. Added together in different proportions, they create other colours. Red and green light together make yellow. Red and blue light together make magenta (pink). Green and blue make cyan (light blue). Yellow, magenta and cyan are called the complementary, or secondary, colours of light. Red, blue and green all added together make white light.

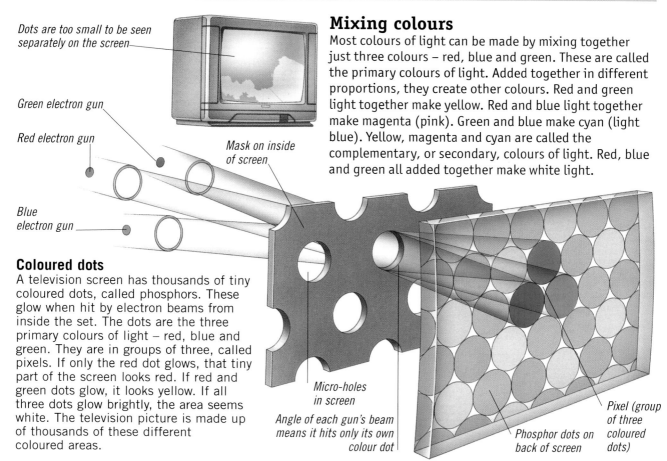

Dots are too small to be seen separately on the screen

Green electron gun

Red electron gun

Mask on inside of screen

Blue electron gun

Micro-holes in screen

Angle of each gun's beam means it hits only its own colour dot

Phosphor dots on back of screen

Pixel (group of three coloured dots)

Coloured dots

A television screen has thousands of tiny coloured dots, called phosphors. These glow when hit by electron beams from inside the set. The dots are the three primary colours of light – red, blue and green. They are in groups of three, called pixels. If only the red dot glows, that tiny part of the screen looks red. If red and green dots glow, it looks yellow. If all three dots glow brightly, the area seems white. The television picture is made up of thousands of these different coloured areas.

Reflected light

WHEN LIGHT HITS a certain kind of surface, it bounces back from the surface, like a ball bouncing off a wall. This is called reflection. Most objects do not give out their own light. We see them because they reflect light from something else, into our eyes. For example, the Moon does not produce its own light. It shines because it reflects the Sun's light. A very smooth and shiny surface, like a mirror, reflects most of the light falling onto it, without scattering. So it produces a bright, clear reflection. On a rough surface, light is scattered or reflected in all directions, producing poor reflections. The colours of objects also depend on reflections. A white object reflects all the colours of white light shining on it. A completely black object reflects no light at all.

Funny reflections
A curved fairground mirror has a wavy surface. It produces distorted, amusing images. The surface of this mirror curves inwards in some places and outwards in others.

CURVED REFLECTIONS

A curved mirror changes the shape of its reflection. A convex (bulging, outward-curved) mirror makes things look smaller. A concave (bowl-like or inward-curved) surface makes things look bigger. Concave mirrors can also turn things upside down. Curved mirrors have many uses. The driving mirrors of a car are convex, to give a wider view. Shaving mirrors are concave to give a magnified image. You can see how curved surfaces change reflections by looking in both the convex and concave sides of a shiny new spoon.

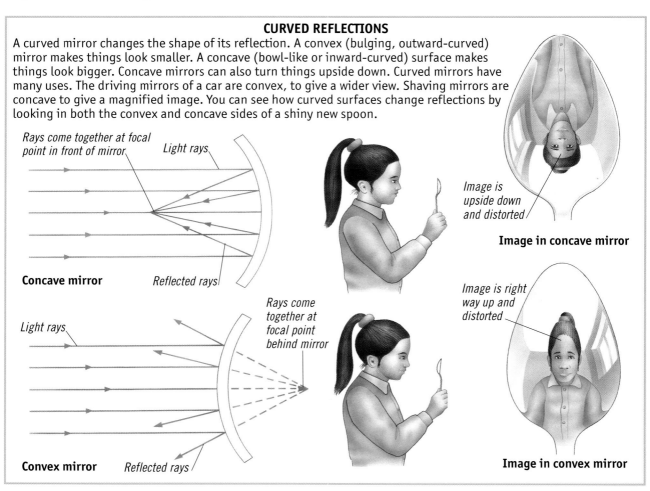

Rays come together at focal point in front of mirror

Light rays

Concave mirror   Reflected rays

Light rays

Rays come together at focal point behind mirror

Convex mirror   Reflected rays

Image is upside down and distorted

Image in concave mirror

Image is right way up and distorted

Image in convex mirror

See also: Light page 74, Refracted light page 78

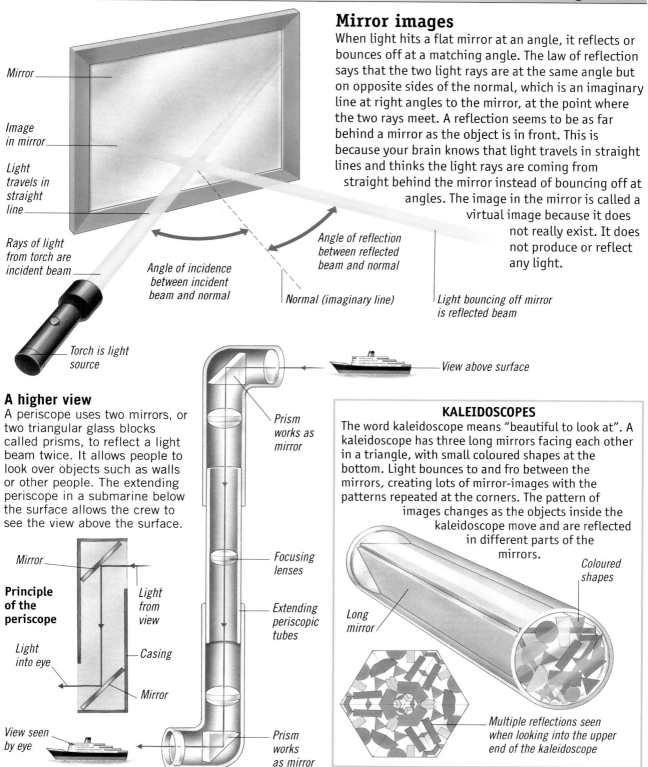

Mirror images

When light hits a flat mirror at an angle, it reflects or bounces off at a matching angle. The law of reflection says that the two light rays are at the same angle but on opposite sides of the normal, which is an imaginary line at right angles to the mirror, at the point where the two rays meet. A reflection seems to be as far behind a mirror as the object is in front. This is because your brain knows that light travels in straight lines and thinks the light rays are coming from straight behind the mirror instead of bouncing off at angles. The image in the mirror is called a virtual image because it does not really exist. It does not produce or reflect any light.

Mirror

Image in mirror

Light travels in straight line

Rays of light from torch are incident beam

Angle of incidence between incident beam and normal

Normal (imaginary line)

Angle of reflection between reflected beam and normal

Light bouncing off mirror is reflected beam

Torch is light source

A higher view

A periscope uses two mirrors, or two triangular glass blocks called prisms, to reflect a light beam twice. It allows people to look over objects such as walls or other people. The extending periscope in a submarine below the surface allows the crew to see the view above the surface.

Mirror

Principle of the periscope

Light into eye

View seen by eye

Light from view

Casing

Mirror

Prism works as mirror

Focusing lenses

Extending periscopic tubes

Prism works as mirror

View above surface

KALEIDOSCOPES

The word kaleidoscope means "beautiful to look at". A kaleidoscope has three long mirrors facing each other in a triangle, with small coloured shapes at the bottom. Light bounces to and fro between the mirrors, creating lots of mirror-images with the patterns repeated at the corners. The pattern of images changes as the objects inside the kaleidoscope move and are reflected in different parts of the mirrors.

Coloured shapes

Long mirror

Multiple reflections seen when looking into the upper end of the kaleidoscope

Refracted light

WHEN LIGHT PASSES from one transparent substance, such as air, to another, such as glass, it appears to bend where the two substances meet. This bending is called refraction. It happens because light has a different speed in each substance, or medium. Light travels fastest – the "speed of light" – through space or a vacuum. It goes slightly more slowly through air. In water, it is much slower, only about three-quarters of its speed in a vacuum. In glass, it travels even more slowly. Refraction is used in hundreds of devices, from eye contact and spectacle lenses to giant telescopes.

White light (mixture of all colours)

Prism refracts light

Splitting white light

A triangular, flat-sided block of clear glass or plastic is called a prism. As a beam of white light enters a prism, it slows down, because light travels more slowly through the glass or plastic. But not all of the colours in the white light slow down by the same amount. Those with shorter waves slow down more than the colours with longer waves. This makes the colours separate into a spectrum. Red light, with the longest waves, slows down the least and so bends or refracts the least.

Clear glass prism

Light refracts as it enters the prism

Light refracts again when leaving the prism

Violet light is slowed the most and so refracts the most

Red light is slowed the least and so is refracted the least

Raindrop "prism"

White light from the Sun

Refracted light makes rainbow

Raindrop prisms

In a rainstorm, millions of raindrops act as tiny prisms to break up sunlight into its spectrum of colours. This forms a rainbow in the sky. You can only see a rainbow when the Sun is shining from behind you – and when it is raining!

Science discovery

Willebrord Snell (1580–1626) was the first person to investigate refraction in a scientific way. He found that each substance has a characteristic light-bending power, called its refractive index. This is a comparison of the angle of the light ray entering the substance, with the angle of the light ray once it is inside. The more a substance bends light, the higher its refractive index.

See also: Reflected light page 76, Using light page 80

LENSES

Any piece of transparent material with smoothly curved sides is called a lens. A convex lens is thicker in the middle than at the edges. A concave lens is thinner in the middle than at the edges. Convex lenses bend the light rays inwards so that all the light is concentrated at one point, called the focus. Convex lenses make things look bigger, as in a magnifying glass, but you see a smaller area of view. Concave lenses do the opposite, bend light rays outwards and make things look smaller.

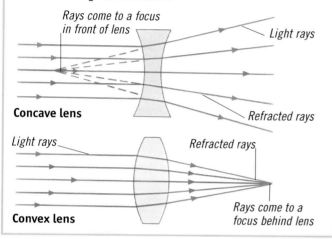

Odd refractions

Refractions of light in water can have some strange effects. They make a straw in a watery drink appear cut in half. If the drink is in a glass, the glass's own refractions add to the effect. Refraction also makes the bottom of a swimming pool or pond look nearer than it really is.

Ripple effect

Water's smooth surface works like a mirror to reflect light from above. It also refracts light from below, coming from objects in the water out into the air. The ripples on the water's surface have two effects. They cause reflections from the surface to be distorted. They also distort the refractions.

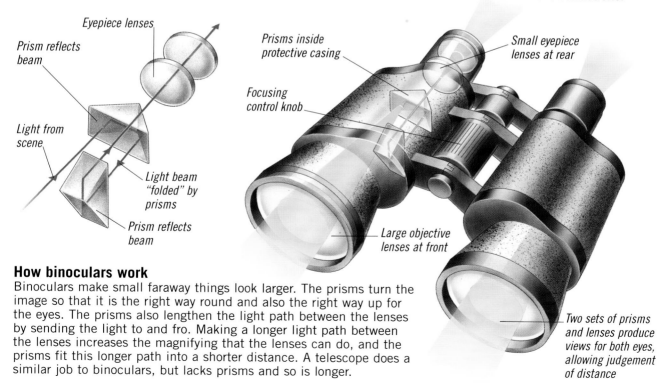

How binoculars work

Binoculars make small faraway things look larger. The prisms turn the image so that it is the right way round and also the right way up for the eyes. The prisms also lengthen the light path between the lenses by sending the light to and fro. Making a longer light path between the lenses increases the magnifying that the lenses can do, and the prisms fit this longer path into a shorter distance. A telescope does a similar job to binoculars, but lacks prisms and so is longer.

Using light

ELECTRIC LIGHTS, MICROSCOPES, telescopes, televisions, cameras, solar panels – we use light in hundreds of ways every day (and night). Artificial lights are especially important at night in our homes, on vehicles, for advertising and to help the emergency services. Optical instruments use lenses and mirrors to change the sizes of images and make them clearer. Flashes of light can also be used to send messages. These vary from the simple on-off pattern of a torch beam, to the millions of flashes per second of laser light in optical fibres, carrying information for television programmes, telephone calls and computer communications.

The microscope

A light microscope uses two sets of lenses to make very small objects look hundreds of times bigger than they really are. A compound microscope magnifies in two stages. Light from a mirror reflects up and through the object (which must be very thin and partly transparent) into the powerful objective lens. This gives the first magnification. The eyepiece lens then enlarges this further, like a magnifying glass.

Eyepiece lenses

Barrel

Focusing knob

Fine-focus knob

Objective lenses

Tilt adjustment

Heavy base

Rotating turret

Other objective lenses for different magnifications

Object on piece of glass (glass slide)

Mirror reflects light up through object

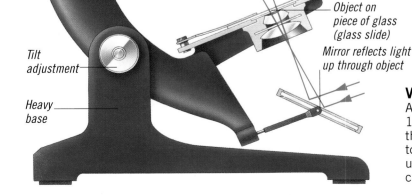

Dust-sized grains of plant pollen seen under the light microscope

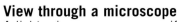

View through a microscope

A light microscope can magnify objects to 1,000 or perhaps 2,000 times. More than this, and the image is too faint and blurred to be useful. An electron microscope, which uses beams of electrons instead of light rays, can produce much greater magnifications.

See also: Communications page 62

TELESCOPES

Telescopes give close-up views of distant objects, from a satellite or space station orbiting the Earth, to stars and galaxies billions of kilometres away in deep space. Because very large glass lenses tend to have tiny flaws, most modern astronomical telescopes use mirrors. They are called reflector telescopes. The largest mirrors are more than 5 metres across.

In a refracting telescope, two lenses or sets of lenses refract or bend the light rays. A large lens at the front collects and focuses the faint light. A smaller eyepiece lens makes the image larger so it can be seen more clearly.

Reflecting telescopes use mirrors to reflect the light. A large concave (dished) mirror collects and concentrates the light rays. A second mirror reflects the light onto a small eyepiece lens, at the side of the telescope, which makes the image look larger.

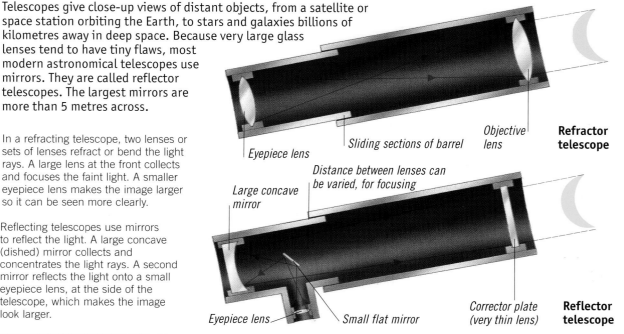

Eyepiece lens

Sliding sections of barrel

Objective lens

Refractor telescope

Distance between lenses can be varied, for focusing

Large concave mirror

Eyepiece lens

Small flat mirror

Corrector plate (very thin lens)

Reflector telescope

Light at night

Without light, the night-time scene would look very different. People would not be able to travel around, go for meals, carry out work, visit friends and family or pursue leisure interests. Advertising signs would not brighten the scene. More seriously, the emergency services would have difficulty attending an accident or disaster, and hospitals would not be able to treat injured people.

Seeing into space

The kinds of telescopes that detect light rays are called optical telescopes (shown below right). They are usually built on mountains, high above the dusty, hazy air near the ground. They are also sited far away from the bright lights of towns and cities, which would out-shine and blot out the very faint light from stars. Other types of telescopes detect not light waves, but radio waves coming naturally from space. They have large dishes (shown below left) and are called radio telescopes.

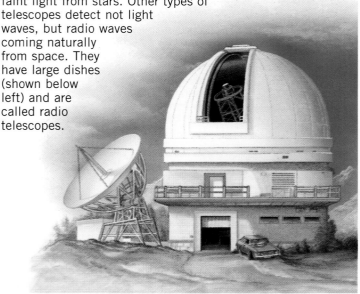

5

Earth and Life

Our home is a giant ball of rock, 12,800 kilometres across, spinning through space. Its surface is constantly changing. Daily, weather patterns move over sea and land. Yearly, volcanoes erupt and earthquakes split the landscape. Over millions of years, rocks buckle into mountains and great continents drift around the globe.

Inside the Earth

THE EARTH SEEMS VAST AND SOLID. But inside, it is mostly molten or semi-molten, and is always on the move. The whole Earth is some 12,800 kilometres in diameter. But the hard outer layer, the crust, is only about 25–35 kilometres under the major land masses or continents, and even thinner, 5–10 kilometres, beneath the oceans. Below this is the thickest layer, the mantle, which is 2,900 kilometres deep. Within the mantle is the Earth's two-part core. The outer core, 2,200 kilometres thick, is composed of almost liquid iron-rich rocks. The solid inner core, 2,500 kilometres across, is also mainly iron and nickel. If you could travel down a drill hole into the Earth, the temperature would soon be unbearable even after a few dozen kilometres. At the core, it is nearly 5,000°C.

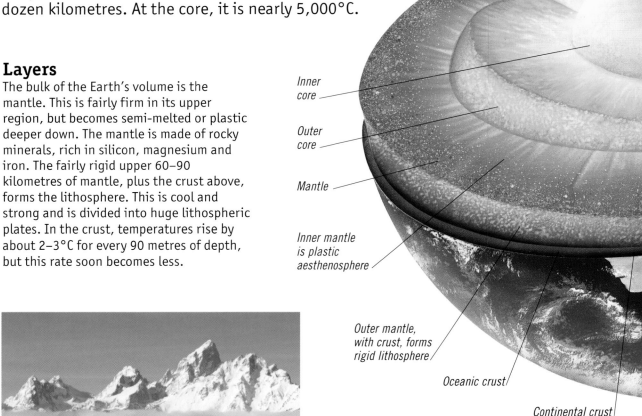

Inner core

Outer core

Mantle

Inner mantle is plastic aesthenosphere

Outer mantle, with crust, forms rigid lithosphere

Oceanic crust

Continental crust

Layers

The bulk of the Earth's volume is the mantle. This is fairly firm in its upper region, but becomes semi-melted or plastic deeper down. The mantle is made of rocky minerals, rich in silicon, magnesium and iron. The fairly rigid upper 60–90 kilometres of mantle, plus the crust above, forms the lithosphere. This is cool and strong and is divided into huge lithospheric plates. In the crust, temperatures rise by about 2–3°C for every 90 metres of depth, but this rate soon becomes less.

Mountain roots

Mountains are vast lumps of rock that project higher than the normal surface level – and lower, too. Just as a thicker lump of wood floats higher and deeper in water than a thin lump, so the mountains of the Earth's crust "float" higher and deeper on the semi-molten rock beneath, than the much thinner oceanic crust floats.

See also: Earth in space page 102

Oceanic crust is young, nowhere older than 200 million years

Some continental crust is over 3,000 million years old

Crust and mantle are separated by the "Moho" (Mohorovicic discontinuity)

Deep drilling

Most bores drilled for minerals, such as petroleum (crude oil), are a few hundred metres deep. The deepest drill into the sea bed, in the eastern Pacific Ocean, reached 2,111 metres down. On land, the deepest borehole went down about 12,260 metres in the Kola Peninsula, northern Russia. The temperature of the rocks at the bottom exceeded 200°C. Yet this is hardly halfway through the crust.

A mere pinprick

Projects such as the Channel Tunnel between France and England are huge engineering feats. The twin tunnels are almost 50 kilometres long, and go down many metres below the sea bed. But this is only the tiniest pinprick in the surface of the planet.

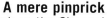

Volcanoes and earthquakes

FEW NATURAL EVENTS are more awesome than volcanic eruptions or earthquakes. A volcano is a place where red-hot liquid rock (magma) from the Earth's interior melts through the crust and erupts on the surface. Earthquakes are the shock waves from a sudden movement at a crack in the Earth's crust. Both volcanoes and earthquakes are terrifyingly unpredictable. But they do not happen anywhere. Most occur in zones that coincide with the cracks between the massive tectonic plates that make up the Earth's surface.

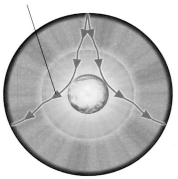

P-waves pass deep into Earth and reflect off core

Fissures open

Plates slide sideways

How an earthquake happens

Most earthquakes start because tectonic plates sometimes snag or stick as they slide past each other. For a while, the rocks on either side of the crack bend and stretch. Then all of a sudden they snap or slip, sending shock waves called seismic waves shuddering through the ground.

S-waves pass through mantle and curve to surface

HOW BIG IS AN EARTHQUAKE?

There are several ways of recording the size or power of an earthquake. Most widely used is the Richter scale, which depends on the height of the waves recorded on a seismometer – a device that detects vibrations of the ground. But a quake that measures 6 on the Richter scale has different effects depending on the type of ground. It causes more damage where buildings have their foundations in soil or soft rock than where they are built on hard bedrock. The modified Mercalli scale (below) shows the severity of an earthquake by its effects.

Seismic waves recorded on seismometer

2 Felt by a few, slight effects

6 Felt by all, some damage

8 Large-scale structural damage

11 Broad cracks, buildings flattened

Seismic waves

Most seismic waves travel through the ground at 20 times the speed of sound. They are at their most powerful near the quake's focus or hypocentre – the place underground where it begins. The site on the surface above is the epicentre. Their power gradually dwindles as they move farther out.

See also: Inside the Earth page 84

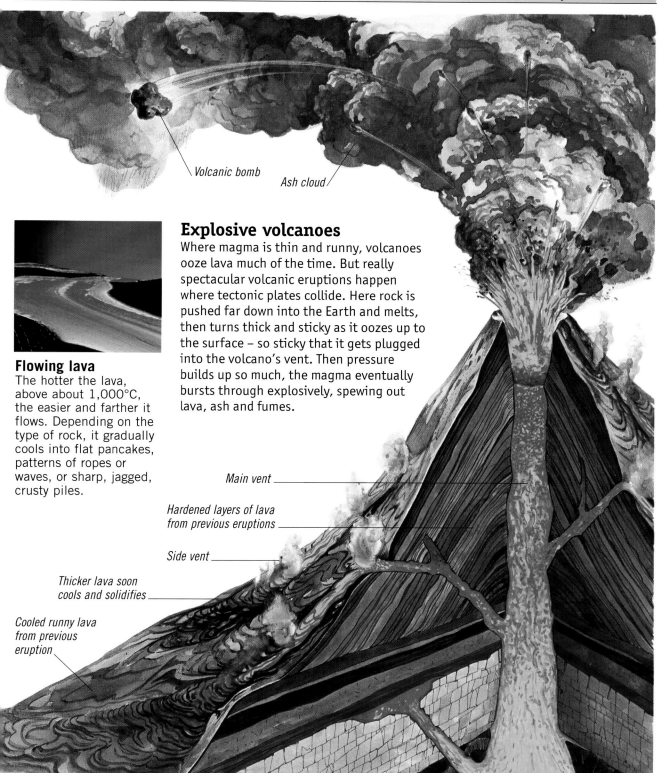

Volcanic bomb

Ash cloud

Flowing lava
The hotter the lava, above about 1,000°C, the easier and farther it flows. Depending on the type of rock, it gradually cools into flat pancakes, patterns of ropes or waves, or sharp, jagged, crusty piles.

Explosive volcanoes
Where magma is thin and runny, volcanoes ooze lava much of the time. But really spectacular volcanic eruptions happen where tectonic plates collide. Here rock is pushed far down into the Earth and melts, then turns thick and sticky as it oozes up to the surface – so sticky that it gets plugged into the volcano's vent. Then pressure builds up so much, the magma eventually bursts through explosively, spewing out lava, ash and fumes.

Main vent

Hardened layers of lava from previous eruptions

Side vent

Thicker lava soon cools and solidifies

Cooled runny lava from previous eruption

Atmosphere

WRAPPED AROUND OUR PLANET is a thin blanket of gases called the atmosphere. It is barely thicker on the Earth than the skin on an orange – about 1,000 kilometres high before it fades into the black nothingness of space. Without the atmosphere, our planet would be as lifeless as the Moon. It gives us air to breathe and water to drink. It keeps us warm by the natural greenhouse effect. And it shields us from the Sun's harmful rays and from meteorites.

Layers in the air

Scientists divide the atmosphere into layers. We live in the bottom layer, called the troposphere. Compared to the rest of the atmosphere, the troposphere is a dense, thick soup, and it contains three-quarters of its gases, even though it only goes up 12 kilometres. The troposphere is warmed by the Sun, but it gets most of this heat indirectly, reflected off the ground. The air gets thinner and colder as you go higher.

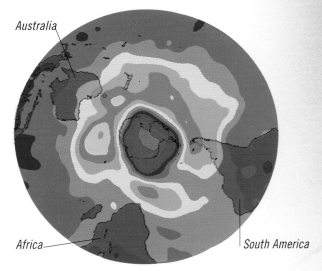

Australia

Africa

South America

Letting the sun in

There is a thin but vital layer of the gas ozone in the stratosphere. So far, it has been enough to shield us from dangerous ultra-violet rays from the Sun. But now it is being attacked by chemical gases, such as the CFCs (chlorofluorocarbons) once used in aerosol sprays and as coolants in refrigerators. Now holes in the ozone appear over the South Pole (colour-coded red above) and North Pole every spring and are lasting longer each year.

Aurorae (Northern and Southern lights)

Meteors (shooting stars) burn up in the mesosphere

Weather balloon

The only clouds in the stratosphere are very rare "nacreous" clouds at 22–24 kilometres.

Most weather is in the troposphere

See also: Weather and climate page 90

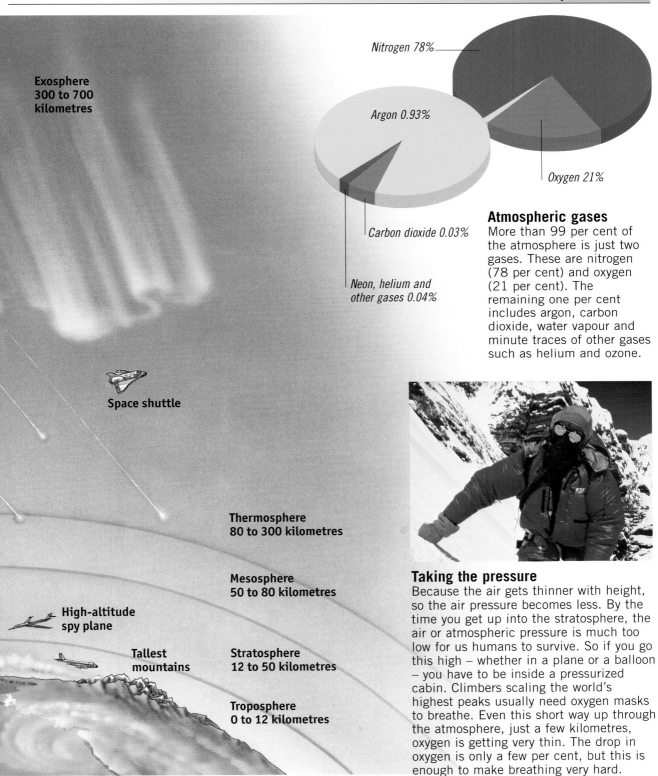

Exosphere
300 to 700
kilometres

Nitrogen 78%

Argon 0.93%

Oxygen 21%

Carbon dioxide 0.03%

Neon, helium and
other gases 0.04%

Atmospheric gases

More than 99 per cent of
the atmosphere is just two
gases. These are nitrogen
(78 per cent) and oxygen
(21 per cent). The
remaining one per cent
includes argon, carbon
dioxide, water vapour and
minute traces of other gases
such as helium and ozone.

Space shuttle

Thermosphere
80 to 300 kilometres

Mesosphere
50 to 80 kilometres

High-altitude
spy plane

Tallest
mountains

Stratosphere
12 to 50 kilometres

Troposphere
0 to 12 kilometres

Taking the pressure

Because the air gets thinner with height,
so the air pressure becomes less. By the
time you get up into the stratosphere, the
air or atmospheric pressure is much too
low for us humans to survive. So if you go
this high – whether in a plane or a balloon
– you have to be inside a pressurized
cabin. Climbers scaling the world's
highest peaks usually need oxygen masks
to breathe. Even this short way up through
the atmosphere, just a few kilometres,
oxygen is getting very thin. The drop in
oxygen is only a few per cent, but this is
enough to make breathing very hard.

Weather and climate

WEATHER CONSISTS OF THE DAY-BY-DAY and week-by-week changes in the atmosphere. We notice it as sunshine, cloud cover, temperature, wind, rain or lack of it, frost, snow and ice. It affects our daily lives, whether we are planning a picnic or piloting a jetliner through a storm. Climate is patterns of weather over the longer term, years and decades and centuries. The climate determines which kinds of plants and animals live where, and the crops we grow in different seasons.

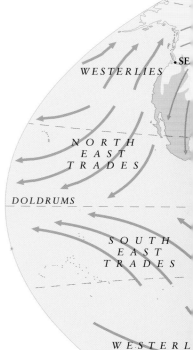

WESTERLIES

SE

NORTH EAST TRADES

DOLDRUMS

SOUTH EAST TRADES

WESTERL

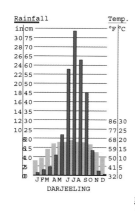

Global climate

The Sun's heat warms up different parts of the land and sea by varying amounts. Since the Sun is overhead in the Tropics, its rays have less atmosphere to pass through, so the heating effect is greater. Warm air rises and cool air flows along sideways to take its place. This large-scale air movement in the atmosphere is known as wind. The waters of the oceans also warm up in the Sun by different amounts and heat the air above them. And the Earth's spinning motion drags the atmosphere with it. The overall result is global patterns of winds in a regular yearly cycle, shown on the right. The main winds are named from the days when sailing ships, which needed the power of the wind, carried cargoes around the world.

TEMPERATURE AND RAINFALL

These charts show the average rainfall (blue) and temperature (orange) for cities around the world. They show different types of climate and how these are affected by nearby oceans or land masses. Seattle on the west coast of North America has a temperate maritime climate with warm dry summers and cool damp winters. Darjeeling in India has a monsoon climate with a very rainy season. Manaus in Brazil has an equatorial wet climate, where the temperatures are much the same all through the year. Cape Town in South Africa and Melbourne in Australia have similar temperature ranges, but the rainfall in Melbourne is more regular each month, as it is in cooler London. Cape Zhelanlya in the Asian Arctic is frozen most of the year.

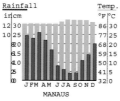
DARJEELING

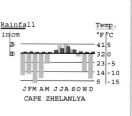
CAPE ZHELANLYA

SEATTLE

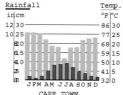
MANAUS

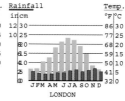
CAPE TOWN

LONDON

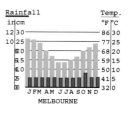
MELBOURNE

See also: Atmosphere page 88

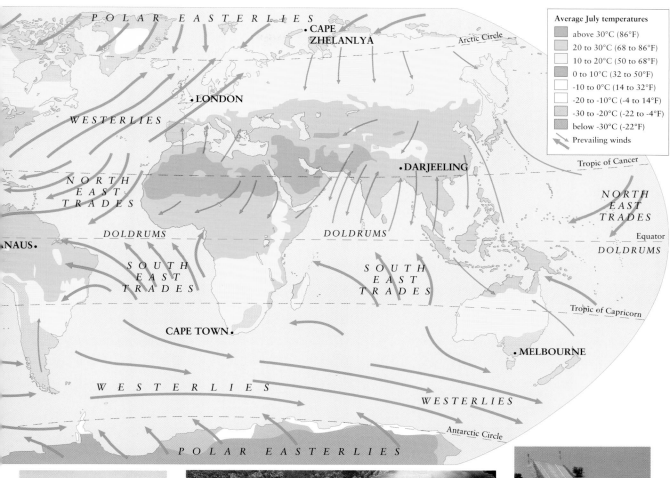

Average July temperatures
- above 30°C (86°F)
- 20 to 30°C (68 to 86°F)
- 10 to 20°C (50 to 68°F)
- 0 to 10°C (32 to 50°F)
- -10 to 0°C (14 to 32°F)
- -20 to -10°C (-4 to 14°F)
- -30 to -20°C (-22 to -4°F)
- below -30°C (-22°F)
- Prevailing winds

POLAR EASTERLIES

CAPE ZHELANLYA

Arctic Circle

LONDON

WESTERLIES

NORTH EAST TRADES

DARJEELING

NORTH EAST TRADES

Tropic of Cancer

DOLDRUMS

DOLDRUMS

NAUS.

Equator

DOLDRUMS

SOUTH EAST TRADES

SOUTH EAST TRADES

Tropic of Capricorn

CAPE TOWN

MELBOURNE

WESTERLIES

WESTERLIES

Antarctic Circle

POLAR EASTERLIES

Drought
Desert regions receive less than 250 millimetres of precipitation each year. Precipitation includes all forms of water or frozen water reaching the ground, such as rain, mist, fog, hail, dew, snow and frost. Since all living things need water to survive, life is lacking in the desert.

Storm
Some weather systems are calm and move slowly. Others are not and do not. A hurricane is an area of rapidly moving winds, 112 kilometres per hour or faster, swirling around a central calm, the eye. This satellite photograph shows a hurricane approaching the coast of Florida, USA.

Flood
Most regions have land that is naturally adapted or eroded to the average rainfall. When excessive rain arrives, the streams and rivers cannot cope and burst their banks. Global warming may cause extra rainfall in some regions.

Rivers and lakes

THE EARTH IS A VERY WET planet, with more than 1,300 million cubic kilometres of water on its surface. Yet over 97 per cent of this water is salty water in the seas and oceans. A further 2.2 per cent is frozen in the polar ice caps and glaciers. That leaves less than one per cent as non-salty or fresh water. But this one per cent plays a vital role in the life of the planet. It is actually never used up, but goes round and round in an endless cycle as it evaporates from the oceans and land, condenses into clouds, falls as rain, then runs back along rivers into the oceans again.

Dried up
Some rivers flow only after heavy seasonal rainstorms. For the rest of the year, they dry up, leaving baked river beds, called wadis or arroyos. Streams that flow all year – perennial streams – rely on water seeping through the ground to keep them going between rainstorms.

Deltas
Rivers often wash along huge quantities of sediment particles, such as sand and silt. But when they enter the sea or a lake, the water's speed suddenly slows down and loses its capacity for swishing along sediment. So the sand and silt fall to the floor and form a huge fan called a delta. In time, the river splits into several main branches as it flows across the delta.

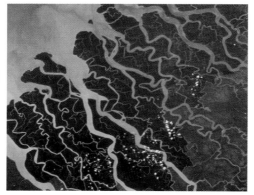

Water evaporates as invisible water vapour

Fresh water runs into sea at estuary

Bogs and swamps
In some flat or low-lying areas, water does not run away easily. Instead it sits on the surface in small lakes and pools, clogged by plants to form a wetland marsh or swamp. The Okavango delta in Botswana is where the Okavango River splits into dozens of small streams and slows down, dropping its sediment particles, such as mud and silt. Wetlands like these cover about one-sixth of the Earth's land surface and include some of the world's most precious wildlife habitats.

The water cycle
The water cycle begins as water evaporates in the Sun's warmth, mainly from oceans and seas, also from lakes and rivers. Water is also given off, or transpired, from trees, crops and other plants. All this produces water vapour which drifts up through the atmosphere. As the air cools, the water vapour condenses into droplets of water or ice crystals, forming clouds. Water falls from clouds as rain or snow, which either soaks into the ground and is taken up by plants, or runs off into rivers, and back into lakes, seas and oceans.

See also: Water page 20

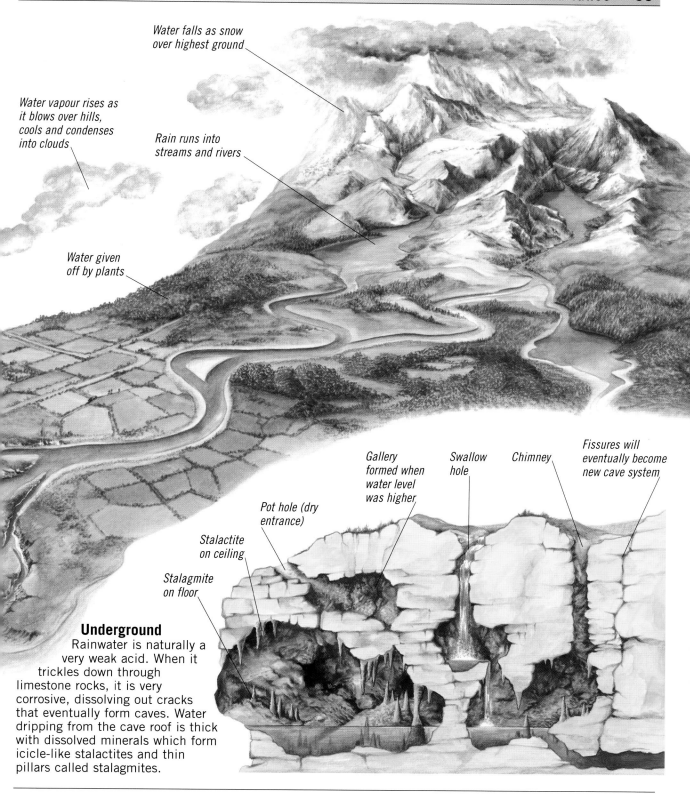

Water falls as snow over highest ground

Water vapour rises as it blows over hills, cools and condenses into clouds

Rain runs into streams and rivers

Water given off by plants

Gallery formed when water level was higher

Swallow hole

Chimney

Fissures will eventually become new cave system

Pot hole (dry entrance)

Stalactite on ceiling

Stalagmite on floor

Underground
Rainwater is naturally a very weak acid. When it trickles down through limestone rocks, it is very corrosive, dissolving out cracks that eventually form caves. Water dripping from the cave roof is thick with dissolved minerals which form icicle-like stalactites and thin pillars called stalagmites.

Life on Earth

ON EARTH, LIFE IS CONFINED to a narrow zone between the lower layers of the atmosphere and the ocean bed. But within this zone is an amazing diversity of living things, or organisms. The total package of Earth's organisms – plants, animals, microbes and everything else – is called the biosphere. It is not separate from the non-living world, but linked intimately with it, with the soil, rocks, water and air.

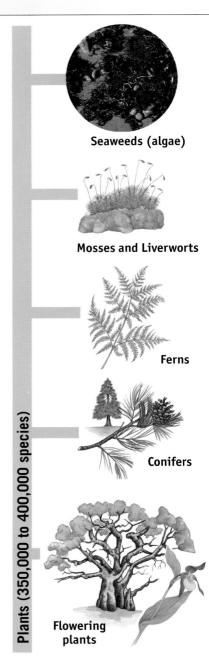

Seaweeds (algae)

Mosses and Liverworts

Ferns

Conifers

Flowering plants

Plants (350,000 to 400,000 species)

How many species?

There are five huge groups, or kingdoms, of living things. Each particular kind of living thing, such as a tiger or an oak tree, is called a species. There are many more species of animals, perhaps more than five million, than in any other kingdom. Only the major groups in each kingdom are shown here. In older classification schemes there were two kingdoms, plants and animals.

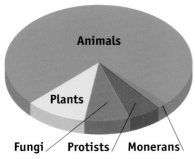

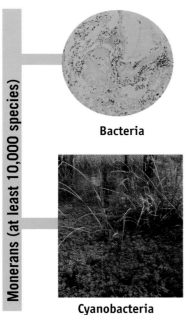

Bacteria

Cyanobacteria

Monerans (at least 10,000 species)

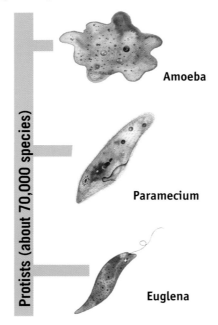

Amoeba

Paramecium

Euglena

Protists (about 70,000 species)

Monerans

These are microscopic living things, each made of a single cell which does not have a nucleus (control centre). Cyanobacteria (blue-green algae) form a "scum" on ponds.

Protists

These are also single-celled microscopic organisms. But each one has a nucleus inside. They include some animal-like types, such as amoeba, and plant-like ones such as euglena.

Plants

A plant is a living thing that traps light energy from the Sun, by the process of photosynthesis, and uses it to live and grow. Flowering plants reproduce by flowers or blooms and include most non-conifer trees, as well as bushes, herbs, flowers and grasses.

See also: Prehistoric life page 96

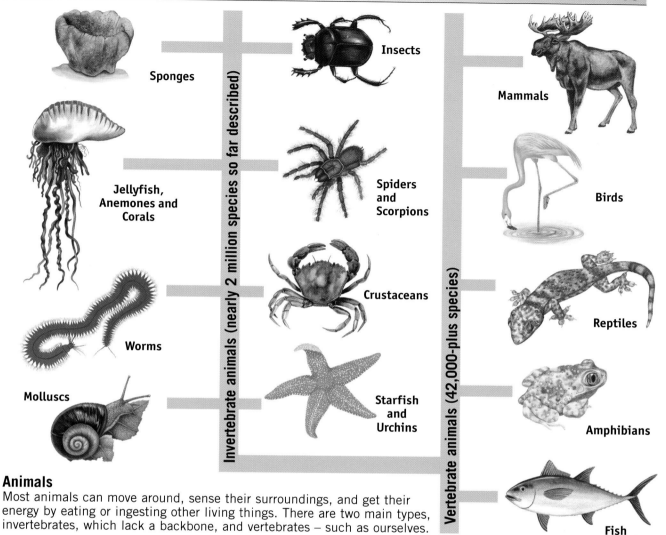

Sponges

Insects

Mammals

Jellyfish, Anemones and Corals

Spiders and Scorpions

Birds

Worms

Crustaceans

Reptiles

Molluscs

Starfish and Urchins

Amphibians

Invertebrate animals (nearly 2 million species so far described)

Vertebrate animals (42,000-plus species)

Animals
Most animals can move around, sense their surroundings, and get their energy by eating or ingesting other living things. There are two main types, invertebrates, which lack a backbone, and vertebrates – such as ourselves.

Fish

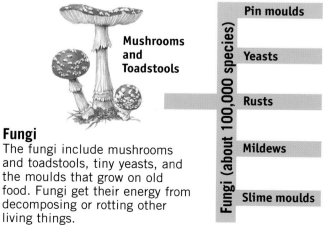

Mushrooms and Toadstools

Pin moulds

Yeasts

Rusts

Mildews

Slime moulds

Fungi (about 100,000 species)

Fungi
The fungi include mushrooms and toadstools, tiny yeasts, and the moulds that grow on old food. Fungi get their energy from decomposing or rotting other living things.

Science discovery
Aristotle (384–322 BC) of Ancient Greece was one of the first great naturalists, as well as being a philosopher and scientist. He spent much time observing animals and plants, especially along the shores of the Mediterranean Sea. He studied the insides of creatures such as starfish, and suggested the process of grouping or classifying organisms by their similarities. He was also teacher to the young Alexander the Great. Aristotle wondered if living things were fixed and unvarying for ever, or if they changed or evolved over time. Most scientists now hold the view that organisms evolve.

Prehistoric life

FOR BILLIONS OF YEARS ON EARTH, the only living things were microscopic, single-celled organisms. Then, about 700 million years ago, the first real animals, such as jellyfish and sponges, appeared in the sea. They were entirely soft-bodied, but rare fossils give us a glimpse of how they looked. Over the next 200 million years, creatures with hard parts (shells and bones) appeared. From this time on, the beginning of the Cambrian Period, the fossil record becomes much more detailed. Some kinds of animals, like sharks and crocodiles, have survived for long periods. Others died out rapidly as conditions changed. Still others have gradually changed or evolved from prehistoric into modern forms.

Fossils
These are mostly the hard parts of living things, like teeth, claws, shells, cones and wood, turned to stone and preserved in rocks.

Geological time

The Earth is about 4.6 billion years old. Just as time on a clock is divided into hours, minutes and seconds, so Earth's history is divided into four huge chunks called eons. The first three of these, lasting 4 billion years, are often grouped together as Precambrian time because very few fossils survive to tell us much about it. The last one, called the Phanerozoic eon, began about 540 million years ago, and is divided into four eras. The eras, in turn, are divided into periods, lasting from 2 to 80 million years.

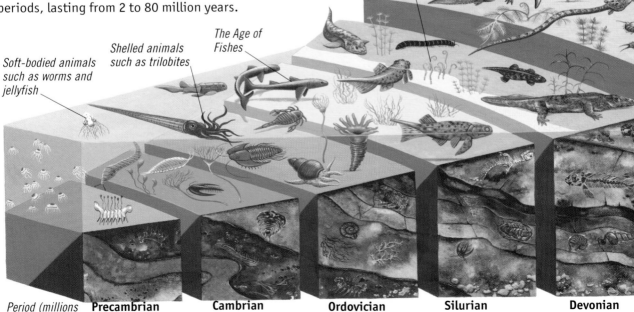

Humans begin about 2 million years ago

Dinosaurs and many other animals and plants die out 65 million years ago

The Age of Dinosaurs

Life comes onto land, first plants, then insect-like animals

The Age of Fishes

Shelled animals such as trilobites

Soft-bodied animals such as worms and jellyfish

| Period (millions of years ago) | Precambrian Long ago to 540 | Cambrian 540 to 505 | Ordovician 505 to 433 | Silurian 433 to 410 | Devonian 410 to 360 |

See also: Life on Earth 94

Mass extinctions

Fossils show that several times during Earth's history, there have been mass extinctions where many kinds of living things die out very quickly. The end-of-Cretaceous extinction involved dinosaurs, pterosaurs (flying reptiles) and many others. The end-of-Permian extinction was even more drastic. Fossil evidence suggests that almost four-fifths of life-forms were wiped out.

Ichthyostega, an early land animal

The Age of Mammals and Birds

Giant birds ruled for a time

Woolly animals thrived during the ice ages

Carboniferous	**Permian**	**Triassic**	**Jurassic**	**Cretaceous**	**Tertiary**
360 to 286	286 to 245	245 to 202	202 to 144	144 to 65	65 to present

Earth in trouble

HUMANS NOW DOMINATE the Earth, and our activities are in grave danger of doing the planet irreparable damage. Our demands on its fragile resources are threatening everything, from the atmosphere to plant and animal life. Car exhausts and factory chimneys choke the air. Rivers are poisoned by agricultural chemicals. Forests are felled as countryside disappears under concrete.

Flooded away?
Global warming due to the increased greenhouse effect may make the world 4°C warmer by the middle of the 21st century. This would melt much of the ice at the poles, raising sea levels and bringing devastating floods to low-lying areas, including many ports and coastal lands.

Atmospheric harm

Two main processes are damaging the atmosphere. One is the thinning of the ozone layer, which absorbs much of the Sun's harmful ultra-violet radiation and so protects us from it. The other is the greenhouse effect, which has always been present but is now becoming more severe.

Sun sends out waves of light, heat and other forms of energy, known as solar radiation

Healthy ozone layer traps and reflects most ultra-violet rays

Thinned ozone layer in atmosphere allows through more harmful ultra-violet rays

---

See also: Atmosphere page 88, Weather and climate page 90

Poisoned waters

Gold is a precious metal that can make prospectors rich quick. In parts of the Amazon region, there are tiny particles of gold in the water. These can be obtained by combining them with the metal mercury. But the unwanted or used mercury is extremely poisonous and washes away, killing fish and other water life for hundreds of kilometres downstream.

GLOBAL CONTRASTS

▶ The average person in the USA uses 34 million kilojoules of energy per day; in India this figure is 0.6 million.

▶ The developed world consumes three-quarters of the world's energy for one-quarter of the people.

▶ Barely five per cent of the world's energy comes from renewable sources such as water, wind and sunlight.

▶ 20 million hectares (an area the size of Wales) of tropical rainforest is felled every year.

▶ Up to 7 million hectares of farmland are lost yearly to soil erosion through overcropping.

Soil erosion

As soil is farmed too intensively, its minerals and nutrients are used up. The roots of trees and other natural plants no longer hold the soil particles together. The soil becomes loose and blows away in the wind or is washed by rain into rivers.

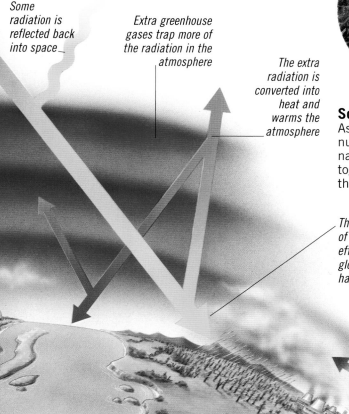

Some radiation is reflected back into space

Extra greenhouse gases trap more of the radiation in the atmosphere

The extra radiation is converted into heat and warms the atmosphere

The natural balance of the greenhouse effect is upset and global warming happens

The greenhouse effect

The atmosphere receives many kinds of rays and waves from the Sun. Some of these bounce and reflect within it, and are changed into warmth. Without this natural effect, which has been happening for millions of years, Earth would be 10–15°C cooler. However, gases from human activities, such as carbon dioxide and methane, are increasing the greenhouse effect.

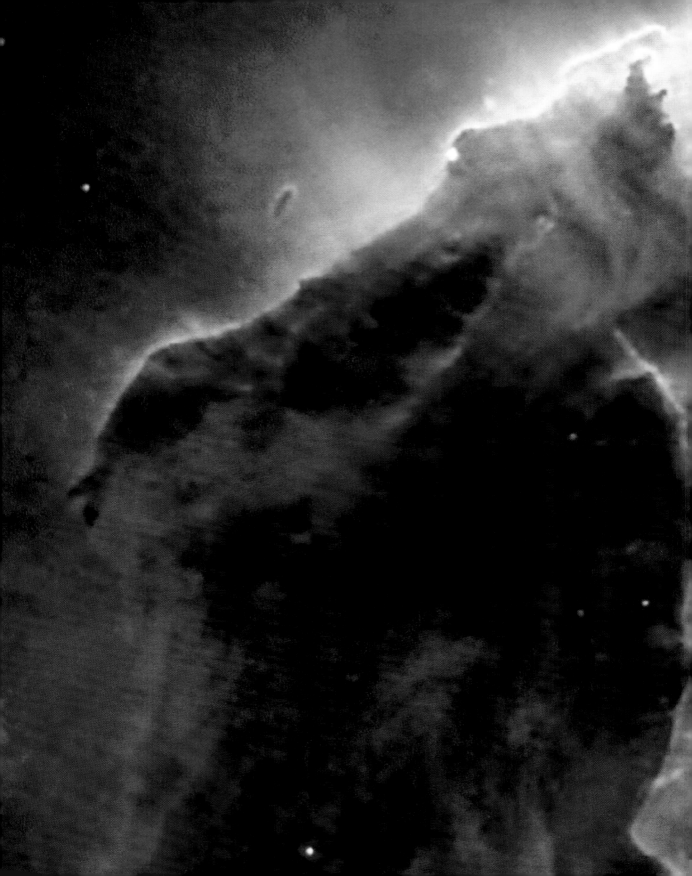

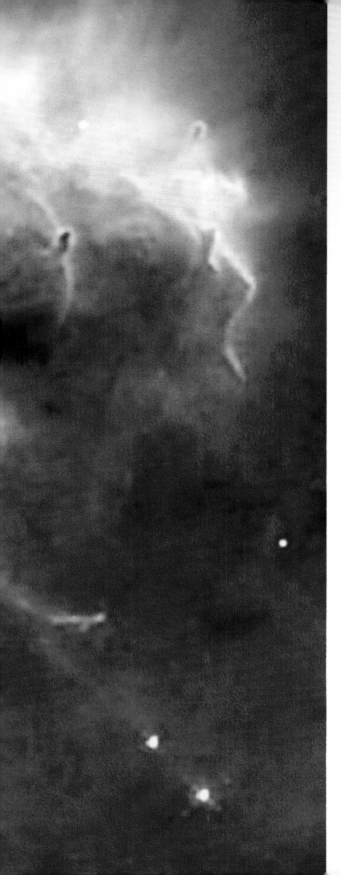

6

Space and Time

Away from daily life here on Earth, the Universe is a weird and truly wonderful place. Stars are born and explode. Star clusters, called galaxies, fly away from each other. Straight lines are really bent, and time goes faster or slower. Modern science explains some of these mind-boggling events – but not all.

Earth in space

IN ANCIENT TIMES, people believed that the Earth was flat and the centre of everything. Gradually, scientific study and exploration showed that Earth was not flat, but ball-shaped, and that Earth's place in space is really just a small planet going around our local star, the Sun. From our planet the Sun, Moon and stars seem to travel across the sky. True, the Moon does orbit the Earth. But the apparent orbit by the Sun and stars is an illusion caused by the movements of the Earth.

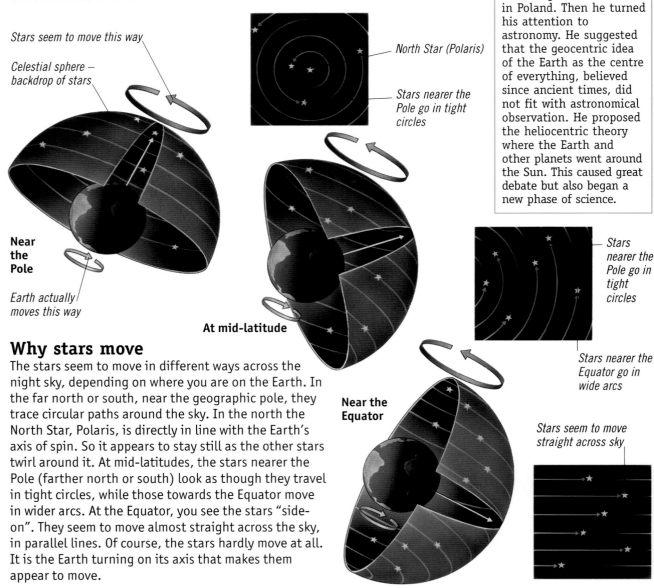

Stars seem to move this way

Celestial sphere – backdrop of stars

North Star (Polaris)

Stars nearer the Pole go in tight circles

Near the Pole

Earth actually moves this way

At mid-latitude

Stars nearer the Pole go in tight circles

Stars nearer the Equator go in wide arcs

Near the Equator

Stars seem to move straight across sky

Why stars move

The stars seem to move in different ways across the night sky, depending on where you are on the Earth. In the far north or south, near the geographic pole, they trace circular paths around the sky. In the north the North Star, Polaris, is directly in line with the Earth's axis of spin. So it appears to stay still as the other stars twirl around it. At mid-latitudes, the stars nearer the Pole (farther north or south) look as though they travel in tight circles, while those towards the Equator move in wider arcs. At the Equator, you see the stars "side-on". They seem to move almost straight across the sky, in parallel lines. Of course, the stars hardly move at all. It is the Earth turning on its axis that makes them appear to move.

See also: Exploring space page 104

FACTS ABOUT THE PLANETS

Planet	Distance from Sun (millions of kilometres)	Diameter (thousands of kilometres)	Length of day (Earth hours or days)	Length of year (Earth days or years)	Number of moons
Mercury	58	4,880	58.6 days	88 days	0
Venus	108	12,104	243 days	224.7 days	0
Earth	149.6	12,756	24 hours	365.3 days	1
Mars	228	6,787	25 hours	687 days	2
Jupiter	778	143,000	10 hours	11.9 years	16
Saturn	1,427	120,000	10 hours	29.5 years	20-plus
Uranus	2,875	51,100	23 hours	84 years	16-plus
Neptune	4,497	49,500	16 hours	165 years	8
Pluto	5,900	2,200	6 days	248 years	1

Science discovery

Robert Goddard (1882–1945) was a physicist and engineer who designed and launched the first liquid-fuel rocket, in 1926. It rose only about 56 metres, but Goddard followed it with bigger, more powerful versions. His work laid the basis for later space rockets.

STATION IN SPACE

The former Soviet Union launched the central part of the *Mir* space station in February 1986. Its name means "peace" and "world" in Russian. The main core of the station is about 17 metres long and 4 metres wide. It was similar to the preceding *Salyut* spacecraft, but with four extra ports where visiting craft could dock, and two private compartments for long-term living in space. The *Kvant 1* science module was added to the core in 1987. Many people have lived and worked in *Mir*, some for more than one year. It is serviced by crew-less *Progress* ferry craft. In the 1990s the space station suffered several problems, including damage by a visiting craft and power failure.

Earth-rise

The astronauts of the Apollo 10 space mission in May 1969 were the first to see planet Earth from another world. As they orbited the Moon, on their preparatory mission before the Apollo 11 landing, Earth rose above the horizon. Like the Moon, the Earth does not produce its own light. It shines with reflected sunlight.

Exploring space

THE SPACE AGE BEGAN on 4 October 1957, with the launch of the satellite *Sputnik 1* by the former Soviet Union. This was a simple metal ball about 58 centimetres across and 84 kilograms in weight, containing a radio transmitter and a thermometer. The world was stunned. Today there is about one space mission each week, as a launch vehicle blasts free of our planet's gravity and delivers its payload into Earth orbit – or beyond.

Launch vehicles

The launcher is the most powerful type of engine available, the rocket engine. It must escape the pull of Earth's gravity, which means achieving orbital velocity – a speed of 27,350 kilometres per hour at a height of some 160 kilometres. Following this path, a spacecraft's tendency to go in a straight line, according to the third law of motion, is balanced by the tendency of Earth's gravity to pull it downwards. So the craft follows a curved path, falling endlessly to the surface as the surface curves endlessly away.

8 mins 50 secs
The huge fuel tank is empty, and released. The main engines shut down and the smaller orbit-adjust engines give the orbiter its final push into Low Earth Orbit, about 120 kilometres high.

8 mins
The shuttle is close to orbital velocity, pushed by its main engines.

2 mins 12 secs
The boosters burn out and fall back into the sea for recovery.

See also: Earth in space page 102

MOON LANDINGS

The Apollo missions planned to land people on the Moon. First to set foot on the lunar surface was Neil Armstrong of Apollo 11 on 20 July 1969. Five further missions followed, carrying out experiments and taking measurements and bringing back samples of Moon rocks for analysis. The last mission was Apollo 17, in December 1972. The next space missions taking people to another world may be to Mars, around 2020. The journey would take about nine months each way.

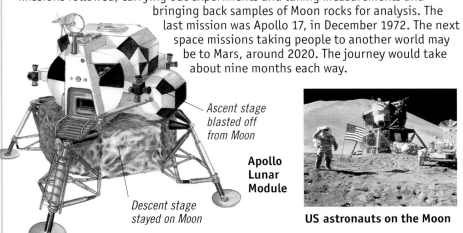

Ascent stage blasted off from Moon

Apollo Lunar Module

Descent stage stayed on Moon

US astronauts on the Moon

Ready for work

The orbiter's cargo bay doors open to reveal the contents, such as satellites. The shuttle can carry 30 tonnes of cargo or payload into space. On some missions the crew manoeuvre near to a satellite which is already in orbit. The satellite is captured and brought back to Earth for modifications or repairs.

Fuel tank

Booster

Orbiter

The space shuttle

The US space shuttle has four main parts. These are the plane-like orbiter with its three rocket engines at the rear, a giant tank containing extra liquid fuel for the launch, and two solid-fuel rocket boosters. The boosters provide extra thrust at blast-off, when the pull of gravity is greatest, and the entire shuttle weighs 2,000 tonnes.

EVA

Extra-vehicular activity is a "space walk". Inside the pressurized space suit, the astronaut has air to breathe, and is protected from the intense rays, extreme temperatures and small dust particles of the space environment.

MMU (Manned Manoeuvring Unit) backpack

Science discovery

Konstantin Tsiolkovsky (1857–1935) was a maths teacher who foresaw many developments in space exploration. He suggested that a rocket engine would work in the vacuum of space, which many people of his time doubted. He also predicted space suits, space stations and artificial satellites.

Earth's orbit

A SATELLITE IS AN OBJECT that goes around, or orbits, another object. The Moon is a natural satellite of the Earth. We have also launched many artificial satellites, usually simply called "satellites", for purposes such as surveying the land, telecommunications, tracking the weather and spying on possible enemies. But the Earth itself is also a satellite – of the Sun. The Earth's spinning on its own axis produces day and night, and its elongated or elliptical orbit around the Sun gives us the seasons.

Autumn in North, spring in South

Sun

The yearly journey

The Earth spins like a top around its axis, which is an imaginary line passing through the North and South Geographic Poles. It turns around once every 24 hours. From the surface, it seems as if the Sun is passing across the sky during the day, and then disappearing below the horizon at night. As the Earth spins, it also whirls through space at 30 kilometres every second, on its year-long journey or orbit around the Sun. The axis of spin is not at right angles to the level or plane of the orbit. This means, for part of the year, that the upper half or Northern Hemisphere of the Earth is tilted nearer the sun, giving the warmer temperatures of summer.

Winter in North, summer in South

Earth's orbit around Sun

Seasons in the Sun
The tilt of the Earth's axis, at 23.5° to its orbit around the Sun, produces seasonal changes on Earth. At the Equator, the Sun is directly overhead at midday on the spring (vernal) and autumnal equinoxes, in the calendar months of March and September. At the summer solstice (midsummer) in June, it is highest in the sky as seen from the Northern Hemisphere, but lowest as seen from the Southern Hemisphere, where it is midwinter. The Antarctic Circle is tilted away from the Sun, so the Sun does not rise in the sky. Meanwhile the Arctic Circle is facing the Sun and so the Sun never sets. Six months later, the situation is reversed.

Low and cold
During winter, the Sun is above the horizon for less time compared to summer. Also it does not rise so high in the sky, so its rays pass at a slanting angle through the Earth's atmosphere. The result is that less of the Sun's warmth reaches the ground, so temperatures are lower. Meanwhile, in the opposite hemisphere, the Sun is higher in the sky for longer each day. Its rays pass almost vertically down through the atmosphere. This gives higher temperatures.

See also: Atmosphere page 88

— Axis of spin of Earth

Summer in North, winter in South

Night-time on side of Earth away from Sun

Daytime on side of Earth facing Sun

Spring in North, Autumn in South

Phases of the Moon

The Moon goes around or orbits the Earth at an average distance of 384,400 kilometres. But the orbit is elliptical, so this distance varies from 356,000 to 407,000 kilometres. One orbit takes about one month. More accurately, it takes 27.3 days for the Moon to orbit the Earth, with respect to the hardly changing background of the stars. This is a sidereal month. But the Moon takes 29.5 days to orbit the Earth with respect to the Sun, because during this time the Earth has moved on in its own orbit around the Sun. This is a synodic month. The Moon does not make its own light. It shines with reflected sunlight. The portion of the sunlit part of the Moon that we can see from Earth gives the phases of the Moon, and the phases repeat every synodic month.

Scenes from space

Satellite orbits vary according to their purpose. A survey satellite that takes photographs of the surface, like the image above, has a low earth orbit of around 500 to 1,000 kilometres. However, this may be elliptical, so for part of the orbit the satellite is less than 100 kilometres high, for a close-up view. A telecommunications satellite may orbit 35,800 kilometres high, directly above the Equator. At this distance, each orbit takes 24 hours. The Earth below also spins around once in this time. So from the surface, the satellite seems to "hang" in the same place in the sky. This is a geostationary orbit. It means satellite dishes here on Earth do not have to tilt or swivel to track the satellite across the sky.

New crescent   First quarter   Waxing gibbous Moon   Full Moon   Waning gibbous Moon   Third quarter   Old crescent

Inner planets

EARTH IS ONE OF FOUR planets that orbit relatively close to the Sun. The others are Mercury, Venus and Mars. These inner planets can all get quite warm – although Mercury and Mars also get very cold on the side away from the Sun, because they have too little atmosphere to hold in the heat. The four inner planets are rocky or terrestrial, unlike the large outer planets, which are balls of gas.

EARTH'S MOON
Most planets have moons. Earth has one, the Moon. It orbits at an average distance of 384,000 kilometres. The Moon is about one-quarter of the diameter of the Earth and weighs one-eightieth as much. It has a similar internal structure to Earth, and its surface is covered with meteorite craters.

Mantle

Inner core   *Outer core*

Lunar craters

Earth
From space, our home would show some of the most exciting changes of any planet, as white clouds swirl in ever-changing daily patterns over the deep blue oceans and the green and brown land. Earth is, as far as we know, the only planet in the Solar System with life. However, some of the moons of outer planets, like Saturn's Titan, are Earth-sized and may possibly have an atmosphere and water that could support life – at least, as we know it.

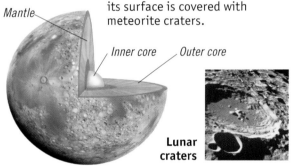

Polar white cap enlarges in winter

Mars
Mars is known as the Red Planet because of the reddish dust scattered over its surface. This dust is made of iron oxides – which on Earth we call rust. The landscape is broken by craters, chasms and old volcanoes, including the largest mountain in the Solar System, Olympus Mons, which is 25 kilometres high. Mars is the only planet to have an atmosphere and daytime temperatures remotely like the Earth's. But the atmosphere is so thin that night temperatures plunge below minus 130°C. Recent meteorite evidence from Mars could suggest that microscopic life once lived at or below the surface, and there may still be water underground.

See also: Earth in space page 102

Venus

Venus is our nearest neighbour, sometimes coming as close as 42 million kilometres! It is wrapped in a thick atmosphere of carbon dioxide and other gases, with clouds of sulphuric acid. The atmosphere is so thick that the pressure on the planet's surface is 90 times that of the Earth – enough to crush a house flat. The gases trap the Sun's heat so effectively that Venus has a runaway greenhouse effect, boosting temperatures to more than 470°C – the hottest of any planet. Venus is almost the same size as Earth, and about four-fifths of Earth's mass.

Seas and oceans are mostly deep blue

Dense atmosphere of gases, fumes, vapours and acid droplets

Surface features are hidden by clouds

Very thin atmosphere of sodium vapours

Craters from meteorite impact

Mercury

The *Mariner 10* space probe revealed Mercury as a barren, dusty planet. It is too small to hold onto an appreciable atmosphere, so there is nothing to protect it from meteors. Its surface is pitted with craters, like the Moon. Surface temperatures can soar to 430°C or plummet to minus 180°C, the most extreme of any planet.

PLANET SIZES

The inner planets are all quite similar in size, compared to the variation between the outer planets. Mercury is smallest, at 4,880 kilometres, and is about one-eighteenth the mass of the Earth.

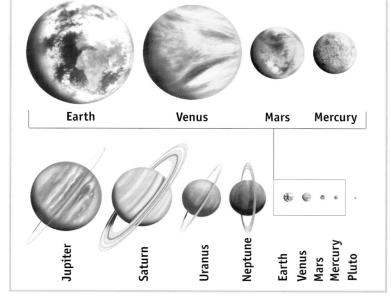

Earth   **Venus**   **Mars**   **Mercury**

Jupiter   Saturn   Uranus   Neptune   Earth   Venus   Mars   Mercury   Pluto

Solar wanderers

ALONG WITH THE PLANETS and their moons, thousands of smaller bits of rock and ice circle the Sun. They range from tiny dust particles to mini-planets hundreds of kilometres across. These are asteroids, the leftover debris of the solar system – fragments too scattered to gather together to form a proper planet. Most lie in a wide band between Mars and Jupiter, called the asteroid belt. But some spin near the Earth and occasionally smash into it. Fortunately, most are so small they burn up as they hit the atmosphere, glowing in the night sky as meteors or shooting stars.

Comet Hale-Bopp
Most comets are too small to see with the naked eye. But in 1995, an unusually large and bright comet was spotted beyond Jupiter, by Alan Hale and Thomas Bopp in the USA. Named Hale-Bopp in the traditional way, after its discoverers, its view from Earth was best in 1997. Hubble Space Telescope pictures showed its nucleus was gigantic, 40 kilometres across.

Inside a comet

The central part or nucleus of a comet is a large "dirty snowball" – a lumpy, potato-like block of ice covered in dust, usually a few hundred metres across. But as it nears the Sun, this dirty snowball starts to melt in the heat. Dust, vapours and gases are blown out in a huge tail millions of kilometres long. Because the tail is blown by the solar wind, it always faces away from the Sun. As the comet passes the Sun and heads out into deep space again, its tail faces the direction in which it is moving.

Nucleus inside head

Head

Tail

BAD OMENS

People used to think comets must be a warning of some terrible event.

▶ A Chinese book 2,400 years old catalogues 27 types of comet and the kind of disaster they create.

▶ When the comet now known as Halley's Comet appeared in AD 66, people believed it foretold the fall of Jerusalem.

▶ In 1835, Halley's Comet was blamed for a fire in New York, the massacre at the Alamo, and wars in Cuba and Latin America.

See also: Earth in space page 102, Inner planets page 108

Comets and craters

Comets follow long, oval or elliptical orbits around the Sun. They come in from deep space, swing around the Sun and head off again, to return years or centuries later. If Earth passes through a comet's tail, the particles of dust become meteoroids that burn up in our atmosphere, as a spectacular meteor shower. Occasionally, larger chunks of space rock do not burn up completely. They smash into the Earth's surface at incredible speed, creating a huge hole called a crater. The chunks that get through the atmosphere to hit the Earth are called meteorites.

Science discovery

American astronomer Fred Whipple (1906–) was the first to suggest, in 1949, that comets had a tiny nucleus of ice and dust, along with frozen carbon dioxide, methane and ammonia. This idea was known as the "dirty snowball". The dust and melting gases account for a comet's huge glowing tail. Whipple's ideas were confirmed in 1986.

SIGNS OF LIFE?

In 1997, scientists announced Mars could harbour life. Yet there were no spacecraft anywhere near Mars at the time. What happened was a meteorite found on Earth was identified as a fragment of Martian rock, knocked from the planet by a previous meteorite. Microscopic study showed minute structures in the rock which could be fossils of tiny life-forms. Might these organisms still live on the Red Planet?

Danger zone

A spacecraft voyaging between Mars and Jupiter has to negotiate the asteroid belt. Most asteroids are far apart, but they also occur in dense groups called swarms.

Some asteroids are many kilometres across

Some asteroids are as small as a house

Outer planets

THE OUTER PLANETS of the Solar System – Jupiter, Saturn, Uranus, Neptune and Pluto – are very different from the inner planets. Apart from Pluto, they are much bigger. Jupiter is nearly 1,500 times the size of the Earth. They all have small cores of iron and rock, but they are made mostly of gases. This means they are all quite light for their size. If you could find a bathtub of water big enough, Saturn would actually float in it. Because the outer planets are so large and so far from the Sun, they are very cold and the gases are turned to liquid or even solid.

Thin ring system

Great Red Spot

One of Jupiter's moons

Rings are only 1–2 kilometres deep

Jupiter

Jupiter is the largest planet, and twice as heavy as all the rest put together. It spins so rapidly, once in less than 10 hours, that it bulges at its equator. Although Jupiter is made mostly of hydrogen and helium gas, it is so massive that its own gravity squeezes these substances into liquid near the centre, with a small solid core. On the surface is a giant storm, the Great Red Spot, which is three times bigger than Earth.

Jupiter's equator bulges with its speed of rotation

Space probes

Several deep-space probes have visited the outer planets. *Voyager 2* flew past Saturn, Uranus and Neptune, The *Cassini-Huygens* probe reached Saturn in July 2004. The *Cassini orbiter* went around Saturn while the *Huygens lander* touched down on its moon Titan.

Charon

Pluto

Pluto

Pluto is the smallest planet, even smaller than Mercury. It is so far away that from its surface, the Sun would look only slightly bigger than any other star in the sky. Pluto has a moon called Charon, which is over half its size. They form a twin-planet system, like our Earth and Moon, orbiting around each other like a set of spinning dumb-bells. Pluto is so small that it is often called a minor planet, rather than having full planetary status.

See also: Earth in space page 102, Inner planets page 108

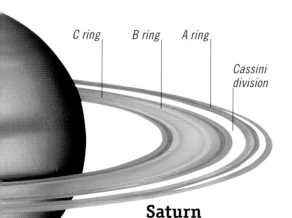

C ring   B ring   A ring

Cassini division

Faint ring system / Great Dark Spot

Saturn

Saturn is almost as big as Jupiter and also made largely of liquid and solid "metallic" hydrogen and helium. It is surrounded by a shimmering halo of rings – countless billions of tiny blocks of ice and dust, most no bigger than a tennis ball, circling endlessly around the planet.

Neptune

Neptune is very slightly smaller than Uranus and equally as cold. Like Uranus, it has an ocean of water, methane and ammonia thousands of kilometres deep around its rocky core. Above that is a deep atmosphere of hydrogen and helium, through which winds roar at over 2,000 kilometres per hour. From afar the planet looks blue with wispy white clouds. Like Jupiter, Neptune has a giant storm area, called the Great Dark Spot.

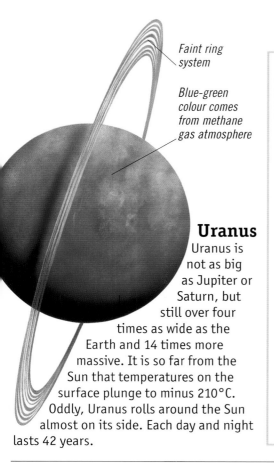

Faint ring system

Blue-green colour comes from methane gas atmosphere

Uranus

Uranus is not as big as Jupiter or Saturn, but still over four times as wide as the Earth and 14 times more massive. It is so far from the Sun that temperatures on the surface plunge to minus 210°C. Oddly, Uranus rolls around the Sun almost on its side. Each day and night lasts 42 years.

PLANET SIZES

All the outer planets except Pluto have ring systems, although none is as spectacular as Saturn's. Also, all but Pluto have not just one moon, but a whole swarm. Jupiter's moon Ganymede and Saturn's moon Titan are both substantially bigger than the planet Mercury.

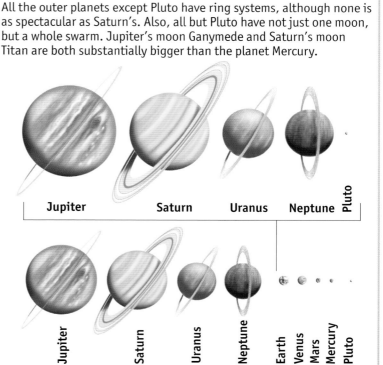

Jupiter   Saturn   Uranus   Neptune   Pluto

Jupiter   Saturn   Uranus   Neptune   Earth Venus Mars Mercury Pluto

The Sun

THE SUN IS OUR LOCAL STAR, a vast fiery spinning ball of burning gases – three-quarters hydrogen and a quarter helium. It is so big, over 1.3 million times the volume of Earth and 333,420 times as heavy – that the pressures in its centre are gigantic. Such immense pressure is enough to turn the Sun into a huge nuclear power plant by fusing together hydrogen atoms, releasing so much energy that temperatures are boosted to 15 million°C. All this incredible heat turns the Sun's surface into a raging inferno.

Corona _____

Chromosphere_____

Inside the Sun

The surface or photosphere glows at over 5,500°C – enough to melt almost any substance. It is mottled with bright spots called granules, where heat from the core erupts through the radiation and convection zones onto the surface. Above the photosphere is the Sun's atmosphere, with the chromosphere below and the corona on top. Huge flame-like tongues of hot hydrogen called solar prominences shoot out over 100,000 kilometres.

Solar prominence_____

Core

Sun power

The light and other forms of radiation streaming from the Sun provide us with warmth and light directly, and light energy for plants to use. Fuels like oil and coal were once tiny organisms and plants which got their store of energy from the Sun.

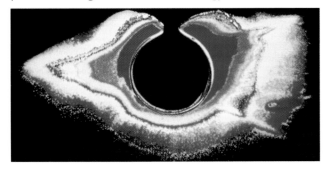

Science discovery

Galileo Galilei (1564–1642) was one of the greatest scientists who ever lived. He made many discoveries about gravity and acceleration. But he is especially famous because he was the first to use a telescope to scan the heavens and make many important discoveries, described in his book *The Starry Messenger* (1610). He was the first to see mountains on the Moon, the moons of Jupiter, and sunspots – though looking at the Sun badly damaged his eyesight.

See also: Earth in space page 102

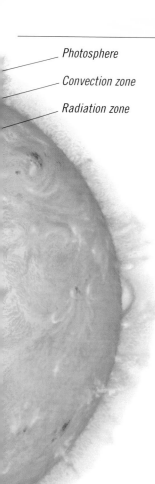

Photosphere

Convection zone

Radiation zone

SOHO
Even though the Sun is fairly nearby for an astronomical object, and also very large, there is still a great deal about it that scientists do not understand. So on 2 December 1995, NASA launched SOHO, the Solar and Heliospheric Observatory. This now orbits the Sun, balanced between the pull of the gravity of Earth and the gravity of the Sun. It monitors the Sun continually and should supply streams of information, coming back to Earth from its radio antenna, for many years.

Solar panels

Radio antenna (dish)

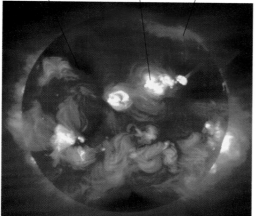

Sunspot   Solar prominence   Granules

Sunspots
Around the middle of the Sun are cooler, darker sunspots. Typically, they appear in groups and move across the face of the Sun as it turns. Their numbers vary, and seems to reach a maximum every 11 years. Some scientists believe they are linked to cooler, stormy weather on Earth.

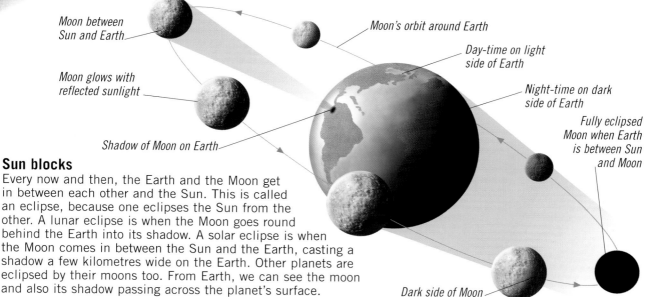

Moon between Sun and Earth

Moon's orbit around Earth

Day-time on light side of Earth

Night-time on dark side of Earth

Moon glows with reflected sunlight

Fully eclipsed Moon when Earth is between Sun and Moon

Shadow of Moon on Earth

Sun blocks
Every now and then, the Earth and the Moon get in between each other and the Sun. This is called an eclipse, because one eclipses the Sun from the other. A lunar eclipse is when the Moon goes round behind the Earth into its shadow. A solar eclipse is when the Moon comes in between the Sun and the Earth, casting a shadow a few kilometres wide on the Earth. Other planets are eclipsed by their moons too. From Earth, we can see the moon and also its shadow passing across the planet's surface.

Dark side of Moon

About time

TIME SEEMS TO BE the single constant feature of our world. The clock ticks steadily. Seconds, minutes and hours pass. You cannot rush time, or make it go backwards. But is this true? Modern ideas in science say: No. Time is not constant. It varies. The faster you move, the slower time passes. There are even theories which say that it could be possible to make time stand still – or even go backwards.

Time going faster?

In the dim and distant past, not much seemed to happen, very slowly. Humans evolved from ape-like ancestors over thousands of years. Then people began to farm and live in towns. Our experiences today are that time seems to fly by, as new inventions change the world almost weekly.

4,000 years ago
People began to live in small huts, then settle in towns. The Civilization Revolution began, with large cities, magnificent temples and other great buildings.

400 years ago

The Renaissance Period allowed science to flourish. New ideas and experiments abounded. The Industrial Revolution that followed, beginning in the 18th century, speeded up the arrival of new gadgets and inventions.

FASTER MEANS SLOWER

Einstein's theory of relativity predicts time is relative to motion. The faster you move, the slower time passes. Astronauts who spend months orbiting Earth in the *Mir* space station come back one or two seconds younger than if they had stayed on the surface.

40 years ago

In a few hours, airliners could carry passengers on long-distance journeys that once took days. Skyscrapers rose in cities around the world. Radio and then television came into people's homes, fuelling the Communications Revolution.

See also: Prehistoric life page 96

MEASURING TIME

Our years, months and days are worked out from the way the Earth and Moon revolve in space and journey around the Sun. Timekeeping devices such as candle-clocks and sundials meant that days could be divided into hours. Mechanical clocks were invented in the 17th century, and gradually improved to the accuracy of tenths of a second. Today's electronic and atomic clocks are accurate to millionths of a second.

Hours
The nearest hour or two can be near enough, if time is not of the essence for traditional events.

Minutes
As timekeeping devices became more accurate, minutes counted, as when catching a coach or train.

Fractions of a second
With electronic timing, one or two hundredths of a second can now mean a new world record.

4 billion years ago

Earth formed from a ball of gases and dust that gathered together in space, got very hot and then slowly cooled.

4 years ago

Space missions were launching many new telecommunications satellites, to cope with the Information Revolution and its boom in mobile phones, computer data transfer and the Internet.

Today

The orbiting International Space Station is being assembled piece by piece, over 20 years.

Mixing and diffusion

As liquids mix together, the particles in them gradually spread out and mingle. This is known as diffusion.

SEE: LIQUIDS
PAGE 16

You will need

2 same-sized jars
Petroleum jelly
Food colouring
Kitchen cooking foil
Tray

1 Remove the lids from the jars. Smear some petroleum jelly around the rim of each one.

2 Fill one jar right to the brim with tap water. Put a piece of cooking foil over the jar. Make sure the petroleum jelly keeps it in place.

3 Fill the other jar with tap water. Add a few drops of food colouring to it. Put it on the tray (in case of spills).

4 Carefully, turn over the jar with the foil and put it on top of the first jar.

5 Wait a few moments then, very carefully, slide out the foil.

6 Look at the jar every 15 minutes. What happens to the colour?

The tiny particles of food colouring are too small to see individually. But you can see how they mix together, even without stirring. This is diffusion taking place.

Making solutions

A solution forms when one substance dissolves in another.

SEE: DISSOLVING PAGE 22

You will need

Salt or sugar
Water in jar

1 Three-quarters fill the jar with cold water. Make a mark on the outside of the jar level with the water surface. Add salt or sugar to the water, one level teaspoon at a time. Stir the water until the salt or sugar dissolves and disappears. Keep going until no more salt or sugar dissolves. Note the number of teaspoons.

2 Do the experiment again, but this time use warm water, up to the same mark on the jar. Does more or less salt or sugar dissolve in the warmer water?

When a substance dissolves in a liquid, it breaks down into tiny particles. These mix with the particles that make up the liquid to form a solution.

Growing crystals

Some solids have their atoms or molecules arranged in a neat pattern or framework.

SEE: MOLECULES PAGE 14

These amazing rocks in Northern Ireland formed millions of years ago when hot, molten rock cooled, slowly. Tall, hexagonal (six-sided) crystals were made as the rock particles formed regular patterns. The rocks are called the Giant's Causeway.

You will need

Alum powder (from a pharmacist)

Medium-sized jars

Cotton thread, scissors

A drinking straw

A rubber band

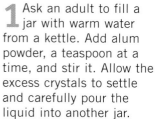

1 Ask an adult to fill a jar with warm water from a kettle. Add alum powder, a teaspoon at a time, and stir it. Allow the excess crystals to settle and carefully pour the liquid into another jar.

2 Tie a piece of cotton thread to the centre of a drinking straw. Cut the thread so that when the straw rests on the rim of the jar, it hangs down about three-quarters of the way into the jar.

Bend down the ends of the straw and secure them over the jar with the rubber band.

2 After a few days you should be able to see some alum crystals growing on the thread. Try to draw their shape.

Alum crystals

DID YOU KNOW?
You can smell things, such as baking bread, because particles from them diffuse quickly through the air. Your nose senses the particles when you breathe the air.

Pond skaters can run across the pond without falling through the surface of the water. The weight of their light bodies is spread between the middle and back legs and is not enough to break the surface tension of the water.

Capillary action

Water molecules pull themselves into tiny spaces and make water creep or flow.

SEE: LIQUIDS PAGE 16

You will need

Water and food colouring

Clear plastic rulers

Blotting paper

Tape, scissors

Surface tension

Molecules of water are strongly attracted to each other. This creates surface tension, which is like a stretchy skin on water.

SEE: MOLECULES PAGE 14, WATER PAGE 20

You will need

Some paperclips

A small bowl of water

1 Put a paperclip on the tip of your finger and place it very carefully on top of the water. Can you get the paperclip to rest on the surface of the water and not sink?

2 Look carefully at the water around the clip. See how the water surface dips down around the clip.

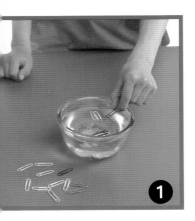

1 Put some water with food colouring into a glass. Look through the glass from the side. Can you see how the water rises slightly up the sides of the glass? This is called the meniscus.

2 Use one ruler to measure the depth of the water.

3 Tape a strip of blotting paper to one ruler about 1 centimetre above where the water reached. Tape the two rulers together, sandwiching the blotting paper between them. Put the rulers in the water. Hold them straight, so the blotting paper does not touch the water.

4 The water should rise up between the rulers and reach the blotting paper. This "creeping" of a liquid along a narrow space is called capillary action. Water molecules cling to the ruler, and to each other, rising upward between the rulers – then through the blotting paper's tiny fibres.

Waterwheel

Make a water turbine – as used in giant hydroelectric power stations!

SEE: ENERGY FOR THE WORLD PAGE 44

You will need

6 screw-type plastic bottle tops

Some bendy plastic, like a margarine container

Waterproof glue, scissors

Stiff wire (as from a coat hanger)

Plastic bottle, with a small hole about 10 cm from the bottom

Two thick rubber bands or some strong tape such as insulating tape

1 Cut two discs of plastic, both 7.5 centimetres across. Make a small hole in the middle of each. Ask an adult to help with this.

3 Push the wire through the wheel and bend it as the diagram shows.

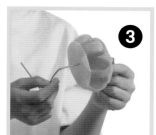

Wire

Water jet

Rubber bands or tape

2 Glue the bottle tops around the edge of one disk. Fix them so that they will act as cups to catch the water as the wheel turns. Glue the other disk on top.

4 Fix the wheel to the bottle, using either the rubber bands or tape, or both.

5 Fill the bottle with water. As water flows out of the hole, it will turn the wheel.

If you put white flowers like these in a glass of coloured water, they will slowly change colour. Plants suck water up their stems by capillary action.

DID YOU KNOW?

Flowers and plants give off water vapour into the air. They suck up more water through their roots and stems, to replace it. This water flow is called transpiration.

Hot-air balloon

A hot-air balloon contains air that is warmer and less dense than the air around it. This is why the balloon floats upward.

SEE: HEAT AND COLD PAGE 38

You will need

Plenty of tissue paper

A piece of cardboard about 45 x 5 centimetres

Scissors

Glue

A hairdryer

1 Carefully cut out five squares of tissue paper. Also cut out four pieces that are more wedge-shaped, as shown below. The diagram shows the sizes of these pieces.

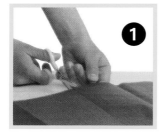

Some sheets of tissue paper are 50 centimetres wide when you buy them.

2 Glue the pieces together. Make a cross shape, as below, then glue together the cross's edges.

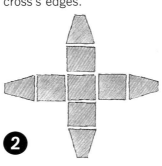

Ensure the glued edges are airtight

← 50 cm → ← 50 cm →

50 cm

10 cm

3 Glue a cardboard ring around the balloon's neck.

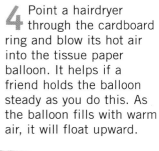

4 Point a hairdryer through the cardboard ring and blow its hot air into the tissue paper balloon. It helps if a friend holds the balloon steady as you do this. As the balloon fills with warm air, it will float upward.

Making the balloon can be tricky. You may need an adult to help. Take your time, to avoid tearing the tissue paper.

DID YOU KNOW?

Hot-air balloons were invented in 1783 in France, by two brothers – Jacques-Étienne and Joseph-Michel Montgolfier.

Aircraft wing

This project shows how an aircraft's wing works. The wing is an airfoil, with a special shape. As the wing moves, air passing over the top travels faster than air underneath. This lifts the wing into the air.

SEE: WATER PAGE 20

You will need:
2 drinking straws
Modelling clay
Thin cardboard
Thicker, stiff cardboard
Paper
A hole punch
Scissors, glue

1 Cut a piece of thin card about 25 centimetres long and 10 centimetres wide. Choose one long side to be the front and make a hole near each end. This card is your aircraft wing.

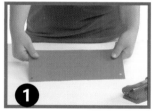

2 Cut out a baseboard from stiff cardboard, about 30 x 10 centimetres. Using modelling clay, fix two straws to the baseboard, so they stick through the holes in the wing.

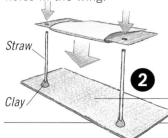
Straw
Clay

3 Aim a hairdryer at the wing from about 1 metre away. Can you get the wing to rise upward? (As you aim the hairdryer, the straws may tilt backwards and the baseboard may even slide back. This is because a force called drag pushes the wing backwards as air rushes over it.)

4 Now make the flat wing shape into an airfoil. To do this, cut out a piece of paper almost the same size as the cardboard wing, but slightly shorter, and slightly wider.

Thick cardboard baseboard

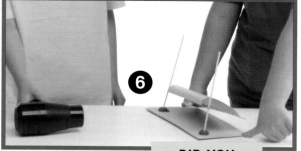

5 Glue the paper over the wing as the photograph below shows, to make the top curved.

6 Aim the hairdryer at the wing again. What happens? This time, the wing lifts up more easily. Can you see how the shape of an aircraft's wing helps it to fly?

DID YOU KNOW?
The aircraft wing lifts because of the Bernoulli principle. This works with moving gases – and flowing liquids too. Try the project below to find out more about this.

Bernoulli's principle

Moving air or water creates less pressure than still air or water. This was discovered by Swiss scientist Daniel Bernoulli, so the principle or law is named for him.

You will need
Paper
A cardboard tube
Scissors
Tape

SEE: WATER PAGE 20

Air moving fast between the strips exerts less pressure than normal, still air. So by blowing sharply down the tube, the strips are pushed together.

1 Cut two strips of paper 20 x 3 centimetres.

Tube
Paper strips

2 Tape these to the outside of a short cardboard tube.

3 Blow sharply down the tube. What happens?

Autogyro

An autogyro is an aircraft with an unpowered rotor on top. The rotor spins as air passes over it and helps to lift the craft.

SEE: ATMOSPHERE PAGE 88

You will need

Thin cardboard or stiff paper

Pencil

Ruler

Scissors

2 paperclips

1 Cut a piece of cardboard 40 by 3 centimetres. Fold it in half. Lay it flat and fold one end over, 10 centimetres from the end. Make the fold at a slight angle as in the picture.

2 Turn the cardboard over and fold the other end in the same way.

3 Unfold the ends to make two wings. Fix two paperclips to the bottom of your autogyro.

4 Drop your autogyro from a high place. Watch it twirl as it falls. The air pushes against the angled blades and makes them spin.

What a drag!

Anything that moves through air has to push the air in front of it out of the way. This creates a force called air resistance – friction or drag – that tries to slow down the object. Some shapes let air pass around them more easily than others. These sleek, streamlined shapes create less drag.

SEE: FRICTION PAGE 42

You will need

Thin cardboard

Stiff cardboard

Tape

Scissors

1 Make three cardboard shapes, each 10 centimetres high and 5 centimetres across. Make one a rectangle (box), another a tube and the third a fish shape. Tape each end-on, to a square of thick card, as shown. Put the shapes in a line. Using a hairdryer on a low setting, point it at the shapes.

2 Start with the dryer about one metre away. Gradually bring it closer. Which shape moves most? This is the

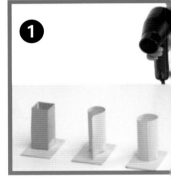

one with the most air resistance, and it soon topples over or blows away! Which shape has the least air resistance, creates the least drag, and stays standing longest?

This is a real-life autogyro. It looks like a helicopter, but it works in a different way. Instead of having a motor to turn the big rotor on top, the autogyro has a propeller at the back to push it along. It is this forward movement that makes the rotors turn.

Wind generator

A wind generator uses the wind to turn its blades or sails and drive a generator, to make electricity. Make blades that also turn in the wind, like those of a wind generator.

SEE: ENERGY FOR THE WORLD PAGE 44

You will need

A large plastic drinks bottle
A piece of thin garden cane
Round-headed map pins
A stapler
Scissors
Tape

1 Ask an adult to help you cut the top and bottom off the bottle to make a tube. Take care when you are cutting plastic as the edges can be sharp. Cut the tube in half lengthwise

4 Put a round-headed map pin in each end of the cane. Now rest the cane on one hand or finger so that it is vertical (upright). Hold it gently in place with your other hand, as the picture shows. If you take your generator to a windy place and hold it in this way, you will see how it spins around. It may even spin around if you blow gently on it.

WARNING!
Cutting plastic can be difficult. Ask an adult to make the first cut, with a craft knife or safe scissors. Be very careful of the cut edges – it's safest to cover them with tape.

to make two curved C-shaped vanes.

2 Overlap the edges of the vanes by 7–8 centimetres to make an S-shape. Staple them together along the edges only, as shown in the photographs. Leave an open slot along the middle of the overlap.

3 Slide the garden cane along the slot. Tape it in place at each end.

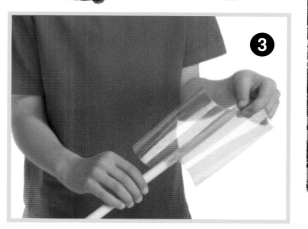

This windmill is not really a mill. The wind turns the blades, or sails, which work a pump that stops the field from flooding.

Conduct or insulate?

Materials that electricity can pass through are called electrical conductors. Materials it cannot pass through are electrical insulators. This is how you find out if a material is a conductor or not.

SEE: FLOWING ELECTRICITY PAGE 52

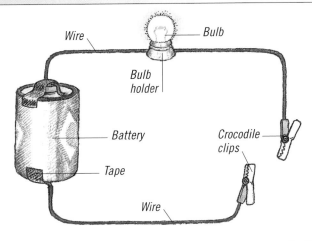

Wire — Bulb

Bulb holder

Battery

Tape

Crocodile clips

Wire

You will need

A battery (for a torch or a radio)

Bell wire (thin, insulated wire)

Scissors

Tape

A bulb and a bulb holder

Crocodile clips

Selection of objects and materials to test

1 Cut three pieces of wire about 50 centimetres long. Ask an adult to help you strip the plastic covering off the ends of each piece, so that the wires are bare. Put the bulb in the bulb holder.

2 Set up a circuit like the one shown above.

3 Put different objects or materials between the crocodile clips. What happens each time?

4 If the material is a conductor, it completes the circuit. The bulb lights up. If it's an insulator, the bulb stays out.

5 Try the "lead" or graphite in a pencil. Does the bulb light up, but only dimly?

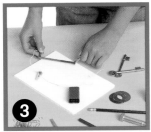

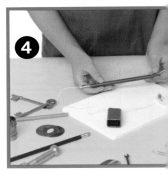

WARNING!

Take care! You need to use a sharp knife or the blade of a pair of scissors to cut the plastic coating away from the ends of the bell wire. Get an adult to help you.

Static electricity

Rubbing two different insulating materials together may produce electrical charges on them – static electricity. This charge can pick up tiny items, almost like a magnet.

SEE: STATIC ELECTRICITY PAGE 50

You will need

A plastic rubbish bag
A soft cloth
Scrap paper, scissors

1 Tear a piece of scrap paper into tiny bits less than 5 millimetres across. Scatter the bits on a table.

2 Cut a piece of plastic dustbin bag about the size of this page. Lay it on the table and rub it hard, many times, with the cloth. This gives the plastic a static charge, which means it has tiny electrical charges on its surface.

3 Carefully lift the plastic and move it near to the scraps of paper. What happens?

Lightning flashes in the night sky. Lightning happens when static electricity, or electric charge, jumps from a cloud to the ground. The static is made when water droplets and ice crystals rub against each other inside the cloud.

Making a battery

Certain chemicals together produce electricity.

SEE: ELECTRICITY FROM CHEMICALS PAGE 54

You will need

Copper coins, zinc-coated nails, cooking foil
Crocodile clips
Bell wire (thin, insulated wire), scissors
Magnetic compass
Salt, water, jar

1 Cut a piece of bell wire about a metre long. With adult help, strip off the ends of the plastic coating on the wires.

2 Wrap the middle part of the wire around the compass about 12 times. Connect a crocodile clip to each end of the wire.

3 Fill a jar with warm water. Stir in salt until no more will dissolve.

4 Put a copper coin into one of the crocodile clips and a piece of aluminum foil or a zinc-coated (galvanized) nail into the other one.

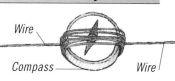

Wire
Compass
Wire

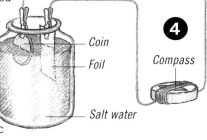

Coin
Foil
Compass
Salt water

5 Lower the clips into the salt water. If the needle twitches, your battery is making an electric current. It flows through the wire and makes a magnetic field.

Magnetic fields

A magnetic field is the area around a magnet where it pulls iron-containing objects toward itself. The pull spreads out all around the magnet. You can draw a picture of a magnetic field.

SEE: MYSTERIOUS MAGNETISM PAGE 60

You will need

A small magnetic compass
A selection of magnets
Sheets of paper
A pen or pencil

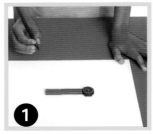

1 Put a magnet in the centre of a sheet of paper. Place the compass near the magnet.

2 Draw an arrow showing the direction of the needle on the paper.

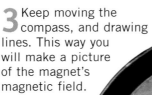

3 Keep moving the compass, and drawing lines. This way you will make a picture of the magnet's magnetic field.

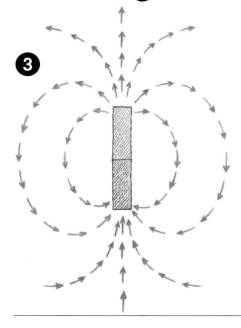

Making magnetism

Use a magnet to make another piece of metal magnetic. Remember that this only works for iron-containing objects.

SEE: MAGNETS
PAGE 61

You will need

A magnet
Steel paperclips (steel is mostly iron)

1 Pick up a paperclip with the magnet, so the clip hangs down.

2 Can you pick up a second paperclip with the one on the magnet? The first paperclip has been turned into a magnet itself. This effect is called induced magnetism.

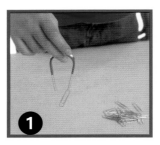

To set a compass, let the needle swing freely. Turn the compass base so that the needle lines up with North and South on the dial.

DID YOU KNOW?
A compass needle is itself a long, thin magnet. It lines up with the weak magnetic field of the Earth. But this is easily overcome by a nearby proper magnet.

A simple compass

A compass needle is a magnet that always points north–south.

SEE: MYSTERIOUS
MAGNETISM PAGE 60

You will need

A shallow dish and water
Cork, craft knife
A steel needle
Magnet, magnetic compass
Tape

1 Ask an adult to cut a slice of cork about 5 millimetres thick. Tape the needle to the cork.

2 Stroke the needle many times lengthwise, in the same direction, with the same magnet end.

3 Float the cork on water. Does the needle turn to point north–south? Check using a real compass!

Radio waves

Radio waves are produced when an electric current changes strength or direction. Make your own weak radio waves.

SEE: ABOUT WAVES PAGE 66

You will need

A radio that can receive AM
Bell wire (thin, insulated wire), scissors
A battery, up to 3 volts

1 Ask an adult to cut a piece of bell wire about a metre long and bare the ends. Turn on the radio and tune it until you cannot hear a radio station, just hiss or hum.

Lay the wire over the radio.

2 Hold one end of the wire on one terminal of the battery. Scratch the other end against the other terminal. Does the radio crackle? This is caused by the changing current in the wire creating very weak radio waves near the radio.

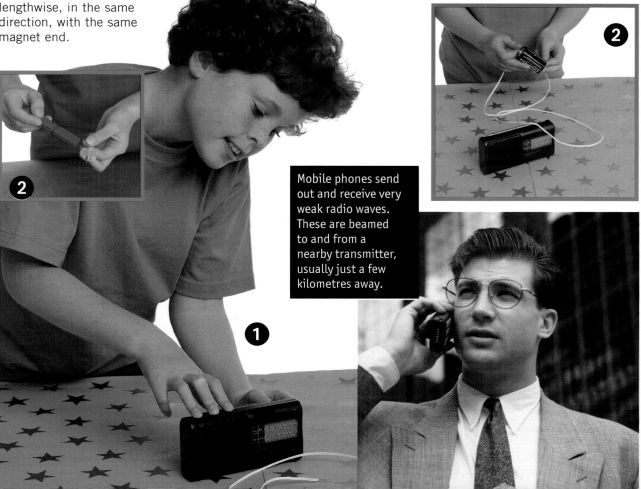

Mobile phones send out and receive very weak radio waves. These are beamed to and from a nearby transmitter, usually just a few kilometres away.

Spreading vibrations

Sound makes things vibrate. This project shows the vibrations.

SEE: SOUND WAVES PAGE 68

You will need

A balloon
Strong cardboard tube about 10 centimetres long
A rubber band
Sugar or salt
Scissors

1 Cut the neck off the balloon. Stretch the balloon over the tube end to make a tight drum.

2 Put the rubber band around the tube to keep the balloon in place. Sprinkle a few grains of salt or sugar on the balloon. With your mouth near the balloon, hum or sing a low note. The grains should jump about. If they don't, try singing louder, or try different notes, higher or lower.

3 Try other noises too, such as beating a drum. Which sounds make the grains jump about the most?

DID YOU KNOW?
Sound travels at different speeds through different substances, or media. It goes more than ten times faster through wood than through air.

Waves in a tray

Sound travels as waves, similar to waves of water.

SEE: ABOUT WAVES PAGE 66

You will need

A large high-sided tray
Water

1 Carefully fill the tray with water until the surface is about a centimetre from the top.

2 Put a finger tip into the water in the centre of the tray and let the water settle. Now pull your finger out quickly and watch how waves spread out in a circle – like sound waves in air.

3 Let the water settle again. When it is still, lift one end of the tray very slightly, and let it fall back. Watch as waves of water travel up and down the tray, reflecting (bouncing back) off each end.

Two-ear hearing

Having two ears helps to locate the direction of a sound.

SEE: LOUD AND SOFT SOUNDS PAGE 72

You will need
A blindfold
Several friends

1 Listening to sounds with two ears is called stereo (stereophonic) hearing. Ask your friends to stand around you in a circle, about 3 metres away from you. Put on the blindfold.

2 Cover one ear, so that you can only hear with the other. Ask your friends to clap lightly, each in turn.

3 Try pointing to where each clapping comes from. Your friends can move around the circle to confuse you!

4 Try again, but leave both ears uncovered. You should be able to point much more accurately each time you hear a clap.

❷

❸

Bats send out high-pitched sounds as they fly in the dark. The echoes help them to detect objects to avoid or insects to eat.

Waves in the sea travel along the surface of the water in a rippling up-and-down movement, until they crash on the shore. Sound also travels in waves, though you cannot see them. A wave is a way of carrying energy, such as sound or light, from one place to another.

How deep?

When light passes from air into water, it is refracted (it changes direction).

SEE: REFRACTED LIGHT PAGE 78

You will need

A glass tumbler of water

A coin

1 Put a coin in the bottom of the tumbler.

2 Look down through the water. Move your finger up and down outside the tumbler until it seems to be level with the coin. The look from the side. Is it level with the coin? In fact, the

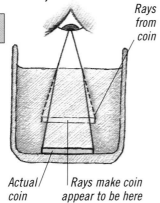

Rays from coin

Actual coin

Rays make coin appear to be here

coin will seem to be less deep in the water than it really is.

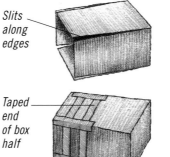

Camera in a box

Try making a camera obscura – a camera with no film. It collects light from a scene and creates an image on a screen.

SEE: REFRACTED LIGHT PAGE 78

You will need

A small cardboard box

A magnifying glass

Tracing paper

Scissors, tape

1 First, you need to find the focal length of the lens in your magnifying glass. In a big room, hold the lens about 3 centimetres from a window.

2 Move your hand until the lens makes a clear image of the scene outside on your palm. The distance between the lens and the palm of your hand is the focal length of the lens.

3 The cardboard box should be a few centimetres longer than the focal length of the lens.

Cut around the centre of the box to make two halves.

3 Cut along the edges of one side so that it slides into the other half. Fix the new edges together with tape, as below.

4 Cut a large hole in the end of the other box half. Cover it with tracing paper.

Hole in end of box

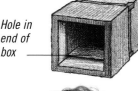

Slits along edges

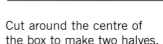

Taped end of box half

One half of box slides into other half

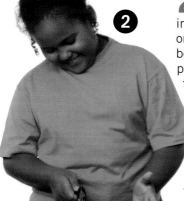

2

5 Cut a hole slightly smaller than the magnifying glass in the end of the other box half. Tape the magnifying glass into it.

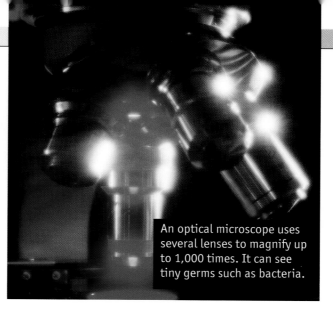

An optical microscope uses several lenses to magnify up to 1,000 times. It can see tiny germs such as bacteria.

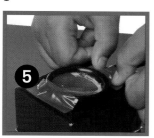

6 Aim the camera at a bright object. Move the two box halves together or apart until you get a clear image of the object on the tracing paper screen. This is called focusing the camera.

Water-drop microscope

Lenses make objects look bigger or nearer than they really are. You can make a simple microscope from a drop of water!

SEE: USING LIGHT PAGE 80

You will need

A plastic drinks bottle
A small box, such as a paper tissues box
A hole punch
Scissors, tape
Water

1 Ask an adult to help you cut a narrow strip of thin plastic, about 10 x 3 centimetres, from the bottle. Using a hole punch, make a hole close to one end of the strip. Next, tape the strip firmly to a small box so that the end with the hole is hanging over the side of the box.

2 Use your finger to put a drop or blob of water into the hole. It should form a curved lens shape in the hole.

3 To use the microscope, put your eye close to the water lens. Hold an object under it. Move the object up and down (focusing) until you can see the object clearly.

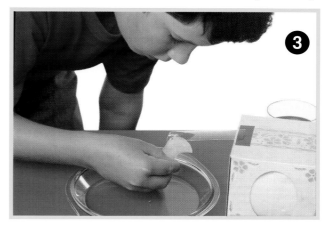

Light for growth

Plants use the energy in light to make their food. Find out what happens if plants are kept in the dark!

SEE: LIFE ON EARTH
PAGE 94

You will need

Cress seeds

Potting compost

A shallow tray for growing seeds

Cardboard and scissors

1 Fill the tray with potting compost. Sprinkle cress seeds on the surface and water them gently.

2 Leave the tray on a window sill, where it will get plenty of light. Check it each day to see how the seeds are growing.

3 After a few days, when the leaves have formed, cut a piece of cardboard big enough to cover the tray. Cut out a shape in the cardboard, and put it over the tray. Again, check it each day. What happens to the shoots under the cardboard? How can you tell from this project that plants need light to grow?

Phototropism

Plants try to grow towards bright light so that their leaves get all the light they can. This is known as phototropism.

SEE: LIGHT PAGE 74

You will need

Cress seeds

Potting compost

Small shallow tray for seeds

Cardboard box and scissors

1 Fill the tray with potting compost. Sprinkle the cress seeds on top and water them gently.

2 Cut a hole about 10 centimetres long in the side of a cardboard box. Put the tray inside the box and put the lid on the box. Leave the box near a window so that light comes in through the hole.

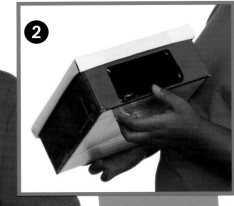

WARNING!
Be careful with mould. If you touch it, wash your hands afterwards. Wash the container it was in when the project is over.

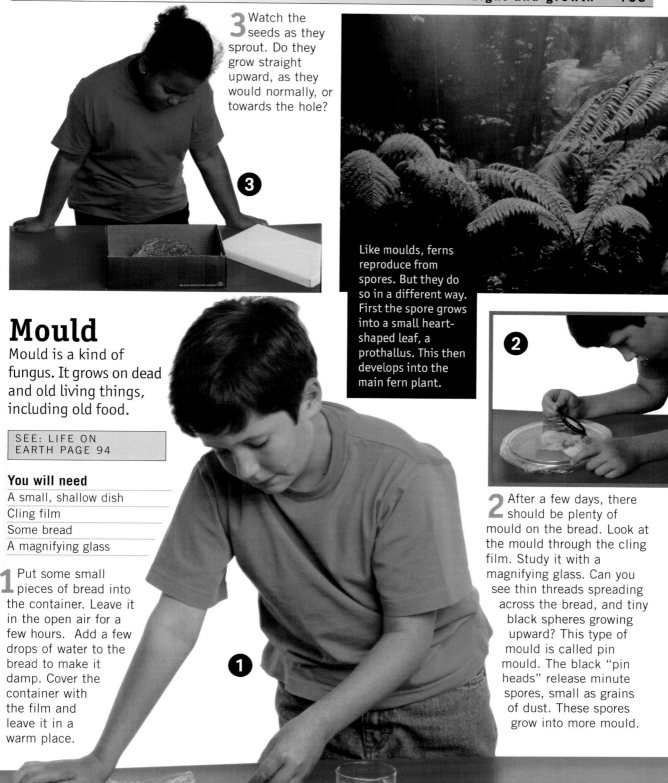

3 Watch the seeds as they sprout. Do they grow straight upward, as they would normally, or towards the hole?

Like moulds, ferns reproduce from spores. But they do so in a different way. First the spore grows into a small heart-shaped leaf, a prothallus. This then develops into the main fern plant.

Mould

Mould is a kind of fungus. It grows on dead and old living things, including old food.

SEE: LIFE ON EARTH PAGE 94

You will need

A small, shallow dish
Cling film
Some bread
A magnifying glass

1 Put some small pieces of bread into the container. Leave it in the open air for a few hours. Add a few drops of water to the bread to make it damp. Cover the container with the film and leave it in a warm place.

2 After a few days, there should be plenty of mould on the bread. Look at the mould through the cling film. Study it with a magnifying glass. Can you see thin threads spreading across the bread, and tiny black spheres growing upward? This type of mould is called pin mould. The black "pin heads" release minute spores, small as grains of dust. These spores grow into more mould.

What does fire do to air?

Fire needs air to burn. More accurately, it needs one of the gases in air – oxygen. This project with a candle shows how much of the air is used before a fire goes out. Ask an adult to help you with this project.

WARNING!
Be careful when you strike the match to light the candle, and don't put your fingers too close to the candle flame. Ask an adult to help you.

SEE: ATMOSPHERE
PAGE 88

You will need
A small safety candle
Modelling clay
A shallow dish
A jar
Water

1 Stand the candle in the centre of the dish. To keep it upright, hold it in place with three or four blobs of modelling clay. Make sure the top of the candle is above the level of the edge of the dish.

2 Put three or four small blobs of clay in the dish, each one the same distance from the candle. You are going to rest the neck of the jar on these.

3 Fill the dish with water. Carefully light the candle and then, very quickly, put the jar upside down over it. Balance the jar's rim on the blobs of clay, with the rim under the surface.

4 What happens? Wait until the candle goes out, then look at the jar. What has happened to the water level?

Firefighters sometimes spray special foam on to a fire. This stops oxygen reaching the fire, so it can no longer burn.

Water floods into the jar, but only fills part of it. This shows that part of the air has been used in burning. The water has filled the space where it used to be. The part of the air that was used is the gas oxygen. It is used in breathing, as well as burning. The rest of the air that is not used in burning is made up of other gases. Most is nitrogen, which forms four-fifths of normal air.

A weather map on television shows where there is high and low atmospheric pressure. High pressure normally means fine weather. Low pressure suggests rain is on the way.

The air and the weather

Air presses down on the Earth all the time. You cannot feel it, but the pressure is always there. There is more pressure if the air is dry, and less if it is damp and rainy. We use a barometer to measure this air or atmospheric pressure. You can make your own simple barometer and use it to help forecast the weather.

SEE: WEATHER PAGE 90

A barometer measures air pressure in inches and millibars (mb). Air pressure varies from place to place and can change even in a few minutes.

You will need

A jar
A balloon with the neck cut off
A strong rubber band
A drinking straw
A piece of thick cardboard
Tape
Glue (suitable for paper)
A pen

1 Stretch the balloon over the top of the jar. Put the rubber band around the neck of the jar to stop the balloon slipping off.

2 Glue one end of the straw to the balloon. Use tape to fix a piece of cardboard to the jar, behind the straw. The card should be taller than the jar, wider than the straw, and not touch the straw.

3 Mark the cardboard to show where the end of the straw is pointing. Label the mark with the date. Do this at the same time each day. Why does the straw move? As the surrounding air pressure goes down, the higher air pressure in the jar makes the balloon bulge up, so the straw tilts down.

DID YOU KNOW?

The Namib Desert runs along the coast of Namibia, in southwest Africa. It has a very strange climate. The air is full of moisture, and thick fogs drift in from the sea. Yet it hardly ever rains on land. It is one of the world's driest places.

Glossary

Atom
The smallest piece or particle of a chemical element (pure chemical substance) which still has the properties and features of that element.

Compound
When two or more substances are combined chemically, so that their atoms are joined or bonded to each other.

Dissolving
When one substance, the solute, splits into its individual molecules or atoms and disperses in another substance, the solvent, to form a solution.

Electro-magnetic spectrum
The range of waves or rays which are electromagnetic in nature, being composed of electrical and magnetic forces. It includes radio waves, microwaves, infra-red, visible light, ultra-violet, X-rays and gamma rays.

Electron
A negatively charged particle that goes around or orbits the nucleus of an atom. Movement of electrons constitutes a discharge or flow of electric current.

Element
One of about 112 chemical substances, such as iron, silicon or carbon, that cannot be split chemically into simpler substances. Atoms of an element are all the same as each other, and different from the atoms of all other elements.

Energy
The capacity or ability to do work – to make events happen and cause changes. Energy exists in many forms, including light, heat, electricity, sound, motion and matter or chemicals. When energy is "used" it does not disappear, it is changed into other forms of energy.

Force
Any influence or action that tends to alter the motion of an object, making it slow down, speed up or change direction. It is measured in newtons.

Ion
An atom or group of atoms that has a positive charge (cation) or negative charge (anion).

Leptons
One of the main groups of fundamental or elementary particles. They include electrons and also muons and other particles. (See also quarks.)

Light-year
The distance that light travels in one year, which is 9,460,000 million kilometres.

Matter
Any type of substance, which has mass and can be detected. Most matter is made up of atoms.

Mixture
When two or more substances occur together and are mixed physically, but their atoms are not joined or combined chemically with each other.

Molecule
Two or more atoms linked or bonded together. They may be of the same chemical element, such as a molecule of oxygen gas which has two atoms of oxygen (O_2), or of different chemical elements, such as a molecule of common salt, which has one atom of sodium and one of chlorine (NaCl).

Neutron
A neutral or uncharged particle in the nucleus of an atom.

Pressure
The effect of a force pressing on an object or substance, measured in pascals (newtons per square metre).

Power
The rate of doing work or using energy.

Proton
A positively charged particle in the nucleus of an atom.

Quarks
One of the main groups of fundamental or elementary particles. Different types and combinations of quarks make up particles such as protons and neutrons. (See also leptons.)

Radiation
Energy or particles which are radiated, or beamed or sent out, from a source.

Reflection
When rays, waves or other forms of energy meet a surface and bounce back again, such as when light rays bounce off a mirror.

Refraction
When rays, waves or other forms of energy bend at an angle as they pass from one substance or medium to another, such as light rays as they pass from air into water.

Solute
A substance (such as sugar) that dissolves in a solvent to form a solution.

Solution
A solute dissolved in a solvent.

Solvent
A substance (such as water) in which a solute dissolves, to form a solution.

Work
A measure of transferring energy which causes an object to move. If the object does not move, then technically, no work has been carried out.

BASIC SCIENTIFIC MEASUREMENTS AND CONVERSIONS

Length
metre *symbol* **m**
Other length units
1 inch (in) = 2.54 cm
1 foot (ft) = 12 in = 0.3048 m
1 yard (yd) = 3 ft = 0.9144 m
1 mile = 5280 ft = 1.61 km

Mass
gram *symbol* **g**
Other mass units
1 ounce (oz) = 28.35 g
1 pound (lb) = 16 oz = 0.45 kg
1 ton (imperial) = 2240 lb = 1016 kg = 1.016 tonnes (metric)

Amount of matter
mole *symbol* **mol**
1 mol contains the same number of atoms as 12 g of carbon-12

Time
second *symbol* **s**
Other time units
60 s = 1 minute
60 minutes = 1 hour
24 hours = 1 day
365.2422 days = 1 year

Temperature
kelvin *symbol* **K**
Other temperature units
°C = kelvin + 273.15
degrees Fahrenheit (°F) = 9/5 degrees Celsius (°C) + 32

Electric current
ampere *symbol* **A**

Light intensity
candela *symbol* **cd**

DERIVED MEASUREMENTS

Area
square metres *symbol* m^2
Other area units
1 hectare = 1,000 m^2
1 square foot = 1 sq ft = 144 sq in
1 square yard = 1 sq yd = 9 sq ft
1 acre = 4,840 sq yd

Volume
cubic centimetre
symbol **cc** or **cm^3**
litre *symbol* **l**
cubic metre *symbol* **m^3**
Other volume units
1 pint = 1 pt = 0.568 l
1 gallon = 1 gal = 8 pts = 4.55 l

Density
(mass per unit volume)
grams per cubic centimetre
symbol **g/cm^3**

Speed or velocity
(distance moved with time)
kilometres per hour
symbol **km/h**
Other speed units
miles per hour *symbol* **mph**

Acceleration
(change in velocity with time)
metres per second per second
symbol **m/s^2**

Force or weight
(mass times acceleration)
newtons *symbol* **N** or **kgm/s^2**

Momentum
(mass times speed)
kilograms x metres per second
symbol **kgm/s**

Pressure
(force per unit area)
newtons per square metre
symbol **N/m^2**
Other pressure units
1 mm Hg = 133.32 N/m^2
1 atmosphere = 760 mm Hg

Energy
(force times distance moved)
joule *symbol* **J**

Power
(energy used over time)
watt *symbol* **W**

Index

A

absolute zero 39
acid rain 9
acids 24, 54
adhesives 25
aerogenerators 45
air pressure 89, 137
air resistance 34
aircraft wings 20, 123
airfoils 123
Alhazen 74
alkalis 24
alloys 25, 26, 27, 57
alternator 54
aluminum 27
ammeters 57
amplitude 66, 72
amps 53, 56
animals
    kingdoms 94–95
    magnetism 61
    senses 49, 67, 69, 70, 71, 73
    tracks 35
Antarctic Circle 106
Apollo missions 103, 105
Archimedes 40
Arctic Circle 106
Aristotle 95
Armstrong, Neil 105
arroyos 92
artificial joints 8
asteroids 110, 111
atmosphere 88–89, 98
    planets 108, 109, 112, 113
atomic bomb 72
atoms 12-15, 16, 18, 22, 30, 38, 39, 52, 68, 72
    chemical change 24, 25
    domains 60
    electrical charge 48, 49, 51
    ionic bonds 14
    molecules 14–15, 16, 17, 18, 22, 24, 25, 30,

68, 72
autogyro 124
Avogadro, Amedio 16

B

ball-bearings 42
barometer 137
bats 67, 70, 131
batteries 54, 56, 127
    cells 54, 55
Bell, Alexander Graham 72
Bernoulli, Daniel 20, 123
binoculars 79
biological sciences 8
biomass 44
biosphere 94
bogs 92
boiling 16, 18, 19, 38, 39
boreholes 85
Boyle, Robert 18
brakes 43
brass 27
bronze 27
burning 15, 16, 24, 136

C

cadmium 55
camera obscura 132–133
capacitors 51, 57
capillary action 120
car-crushers 35
carbon 24, 26
carbon dioxide 24, 109
Carlson, Chester 51
Cassini-Huygens spacecraft 37, 112
caterpillar tracks 35
Cavendish, Henry 25
caves 23, 93
Celsius 38
CFCs (chlorofluorocarbons) 88

Channel Tunnel 85
Charon 112
chemical changes 15, 24–25
chemical compounds 13
chemical elements 12, 13, 26
chemical energy 30, 32, 33
chemical sciences 8
chlorine 22
chromium 26
Civilization Revolution 116
climate 90–91
clocks 37, 117
clouds 21, 92
coal 32, 44, 45
cobalt 59
cold 38–39
colour 74, 75
    colour change 24
    filters 75
    mixing 75
    primary colours 75
combustion 16, 24
comets 110–111
communications devices 62–63
Communications Revolution 116
compass 58, 60, 129
condensation 18, 19
conductors 56, 126
Copernicus, Nicolaus 6, 102
copper 27
Coulomb, Charles 61
coulombs 53
craters 111
crystals 15, 22, 119
Curie, Marie 45
cyanobacteria 94

D

Dalton, John 13
dams 44
decibel scale 72, 73

deforestation 98, 99
deltas 92
Democritus 12
detergents 23
diffusion 118
dinosaurs 96–97
diodes 57
dissolving 22–23
Doppler, Christian 69
Doppler effect 69
drag 42, 124
drought 91

E

ears
  animal ears 73
  human ears 73
  protection 72
Earth 84–85, 103, 108
  age 96
  core 84
  crust 84, 85, 86
  environmental problems 98–99
  formation 117
  gravity 36, 37, 104
  life on Earth 94–97
  magnetism 60
  mantle 84
  orbit 102, 106–107
  seasons 106
  size 84, 103, 109
  temperature 84
earthquakes 86–87
eclipses 115
EEG (electro-encephalograph) 53
Einstein, Albert 7, 8, 116
electric shock 48, 50
electrical cables 53
electricity 45, 48–59
  alternating current (AC) 52, 53, 57
  animal sensitivity 49, 54
  in the body 53
  chemical sources 54–55
  current electricity 52-53, 56
  direct current (DC) 52, 53

electrical cells 54, 55, 57
electrical circuits 56–57
electrical energy 30, 31, 32, 33, 48–49, 50, 57
  generating 32–33
  hydroelectricity 21, 44
  positive and negative charge 48, 49, 51
  static electricity 50–51, 127
electricity distribution grid 48
electrodes 54
electrolytes 54, 55
electromagnetic energy 30
electromagnetic radiation 39
electromagnetic waves 62, 67
electromagnetism 58–59, 67
electromotive force (EMF) 53
electronic circuits 51
electrons 14, 22, 48, 49, 51, 52, 56
elephants 12, 71
energy 30–31, 44–45
  chemical energy 30, 32, 33
  conversion 32–33
  electrical energy 30, 31, 32, 33, 48–49, 50, 57
  electromagnetic energy 30
  heat energy 18, 30, 38, 39
  kinetic energy 21, 30, 31, 32, 33, 38, 42
  light energy 30, 66
  nuclear energy 9, 30, 31, 44
  potential energy 30, 31, 32
  renewable energy 45, 99
  solar energy 31, 33, 98, 114
  sound energy 30, 66, 68, 71, 72
energy consumption 99
EVA (extravehicular activity) 105
exhaust fumes 16
extinctions 97

F

farads 53
fibre-optic cables 62
floating 21
floods 91, 98
forces 34–35, 42
fossil fuels 44, 45
fossils 96, 97
Franklin, Benjamin 49

frequency 70, 72
friction 38, 42–43, 51
fulcrum 40, 41
fungi 95, 135
fuse boxes 56
fuses 57

G

Galileo Galilei 114
gamma rays 30
gases 16–17, 18
  atmospheric gases 89
generators 51
geological time 96
global warming 9, 91, 98
Goddard, Robert 103
gold 26, 27, 99
Grand Prix racing cars 25
gravity 7, 34, 36–37, 104
greenhouse effect 88, 98, 99

H

Hale-Bopp Comet 110
Halley's Comet 110
hearing 72–73, 131
  stereo hearing 131
heat 38–39
heat energy 18, 30, 38, 39
helium 89, 112, 113, 114
Helmholtz, Hermann 31
Hertz 53, 70
Hertz, Heinrich 70
Hooke, Robert 32
hot-air balloons 122
hovercraft 42
Hubble Space Telescope 110
hurricanes 91
hydraulic rams 40
hydroelectricity 21, 44
hydrofoil 43
hydrogen 13, 21, 25, 113, 114

I

ice 17, 19, 20, 38
inclined plane 40
Industrial Revolution 7, 116
infra-red (IR) light 39, 67
infrasonic sounds 70, 71
insulators 39, 53, 56, 126
International Space Station 117
ionic bonds 14
ions 14, 17, 22, 54
iron 12, 26, 58, 59, 60, 84

J

Joule, James 38
joules 53
Jupiter 37, 103, 109, 112

K

kaleidoscopes 77
Kelvin scale 39
Kepler, Johannes 106
kilowatt-hour (KWH) 53
kinetic energy 21, 30, 31, 32, 33, 38, 42

L

lakes 92–93
laminar flow 20
laser light 62
launch vehicles 104
lava 18, 87
Leaning Tower of Pisa 36
LED (light emitting diode) 57
Leeuwenhoek, Antonie van 80
lenses 79
Leonardo da Vinci 7
levers 40–41
light 66–67, 74–75
    colour 74, 75
    laser light 62
    light energy 30, 66
    light waves 66, 67, 75
    reflected light 76–77
    refracted light 78–79, 132
    speed of light 62, 74
    travel 74, 78
    ultra-violet (UV) light 67, 74, 88, 98
    wave-particle duality of light 74
light bulbs 56, 57
lightning 17, 30, 49, 50
lignin 12
liquids 16–17, 18, 118
lithosphere 84
litmus 24
lubrication 42
lunar eclipse 115

M

maglev trains 59
magma 18, 87
magnesium 27, 84
magnetism 58–61, 128
    animals 61
    Earth 60
    electromagnetism 58–59, 67
    magnetic energy 30
    magnetic fields 60, 61, 128
manganese 26
Mars 103, 108, 109, 111
mass 31, 36
matter 16, 18, 31, 36
Maxwell, James Clerk 67
mechanical diggers 40, 41
melting 16, 18, 19
mercury (metal) 24, 99
Mercury (planet) 103, 108, 109
metallurgy 26
metals 26–27
meteorites 88, 111
microscope 32, 74, 80
    electron microscope 80
    water-drop microscope 133
microwaves 30
minerals 23, 25, 27, 84, 85, 93
mining 27, 45
Mir space station 103, 116
mirror images 76, 77
mobile phones 63
Modified Mercalli scale 86
molecules 14–15, 16, 17, 18, 21, 22, 24, 25, 30, 68, 72
monerans 94
monsoons 90
Moon 36, 76, 106, 115
    lunar eclipse 115
    Moon landings 105
    orbit 107, 108
    phases 107
moons 108, 112
motion 34–35, 42, 116
mould 135
mountains 84
movement energy, see kinetic energy
MRI (Magnetic Resonance Imaging) 30
muscles 33, 35, 53, 54
music 68, 72
    musical instruments 71
    musical notation 71

N

Namib Desert 137
natural gas 18, 44
navigation 61
Neptune 103, 109, 113
nerve signals 53
neutrons 49
Newton, Isaac 7, 34
newtons 36
nickel 55, 59, 84
nitrogen 89
nuclear fission 31
nuclear fusion 31
nuclear power 9, 30, 31, 44

O

oasis 21
Oersted, Hans Christian 58
Ohm, Georg Simon 56
ohms 53, 56
oil 23, 42, 43, 44
opaque substances 74
optical instruments 80–81

optical telescopes 81

orbits 36, 102, 106–107

ores 27

oxygen 14, 15, 21, 24, 25, 26, 89, 136

ozone 14, 89

ozone layer 9, 88, 98

P

pacemakers 55

paints 23

palladium 26

pendulum clock 37

periscopes 77

phosphors 75

phosphorus 26

photocopiers 50–51

photons 74

photosynthesis 94

phototropism 134–135

physical sciences 7

pig iron 26

pile driver 35

pitch 70, 71, 72

planets 102, 103

   inner planets 108–109

   outer planets 112–113

plants 94, 134–135

plasma 17

platinum 26

Pluto 103, 109, 112

poles, north and south 60, 88, 102, 106

pollution 9, 16, 23, 98

polonium 45

potential difference 52, 53

potential energy 30, 31, 32

power cables 53

power stations 32, 44, 48

precipitation 91

prehistoric life 96–97

prisms 77, 78, 79

protists 94

protons 48, 49

pyramids 7, 40

R

radio telescopes 81

radio waves 30, 62, 63, 70, 129

radioactivity 9, 45

radium 45

rainbows 74, 78

raindrops 78

rainfall 90, 91, 92

ramp 40

recycling 27

reflecting telescopes 81

reflection 76–77

reflector telescopes 81

refracting telescopes 81

refraction 78–79, 132

refractive index 78

refrigerator 19

relativity theory 7, 116

Renaissance 116

renewable energy 45, 99

resistors 57

Richter scale 86

ring mains 56

rivers 92–93

robots 31

rockets 73, 103, 104, 105

rubber, vulcanized 25

S

salt 15, 22

satellites 33, 104, 106, 107

Saturn 37, 103, 109, 112–113

scanners 30

screws 40

sea water 22

seasons 106

seismic waves 86

sharks 49

shooting stars 110

silicon 26, 27, 84

silver 27

simple machines 40–41

sinking 21

skydiving 36

slope 40

Snell, Willebrord 78

sodium 22

sodium chloride 22

SOHO (Solar and Heliospheric Observatory) 115

soil erosion 99

solar eclipse 115

solar energy 31, 33, 114

Solar System 108

solenoids 57, 58

solids 16–17, 18

solutions 22, 23, 118

solvents 22, 23

sonic speed 69

sound 66–67

   decibel scale 72, 73

   frequencies 70, 72

   high and low sounds 70–71

   loud and soft sounds 72–73

   sonic speed 69

   sound energy 30, 66, 68, 71, 72

   sound waves 66, 67, 68–69, 130, 131

space 13

space exploration 104–105, 112, 117

space probes 112

space shuttles 8, 105

space stations 103

species 94

Sputnik 1 104

stalactites and stalagmites 23, 93

stars 102

static electricity 50–51, 127

steam power 7, 32

steel 26, 58, 59

Stone-Age tools 6

stratosphere 88

submarines 21

sugar 22

sulphur 26

Sun 114–115

   gravity 36

   seasons 106

   solar eclipse 115

   solar energy 31, 33, 98, 114

   temperature 114

   weather 90

sunspots 115
supersonic aircraft 69
swamps 92
switches 56, 57

T

tectonic plates 86, 87
telephones 62, 63, 80
telescopes 79, 81
television 62, 63, 75, 80
temperature 38, 39, 90
Tesla, Nikola 52
Tesla coil 52
thermocouple 38
thermodynamics 38
tidal energy 45
time 116–117
  geological time 96
  timekeeping 117
tin 27
Titan 108, 112
titanium 26, 38
torches 56, 80
transformers 57
transistors 57
translucent substances 74
transparent substances 16, 74, 78
troposphere 88
Tsiolkovsky, Konstantin 105

U

ultrasonic sounds 67, 70
ultraviolet (UV) light 67, 74, 88, 98
uranium 45
Uranus 103, 109, 113

V

vacuum 66
Venus 37, 103, 108, 109
vibrations 68, 130
volcanoes 18, 86–87
Volta, Alessandro 55
Voltaic pile 55

voltmeter 57
volts 53, 54

W

wadis 92
water 17, 20–21, 25
  boiling point 18, 39
  capillary action 120
  hydroelectricity 21, 44
  molecules 21
  solvent 22, 23
  speed of flow 20
  surface tension 120
  water cycle 92–93
  water vapor 17, 20, 92
waterwheel 121
watts 53
wave energy 45
wavelength 66
waves
  electromagnetic waves 62, 67
  frequencies 66
  light waves 66, 67, 75
  radio waves 30, 62, 63, 70, 129
  seismic waves 86
  sound waves 66, 67, 68–69, 130, 131
weather 90–91, 137
wedges 40, 41
weight 36
wetlands 92
whales 69, 72
Whipple, Fred 111
wind farms 45
wind generator 125
windmills 44
winds 44, 90

X

X-rays 30

Z

Zworykin, Vladimir 63